CALVIN'S DOXOLOGY

Worship in the 1559 *Institutes* with a View to Contemporary Worship Renewal

Pamela Ann Moeller

PICKWICK PUBLICATIONS
ALLISON PARK, PENNSYLVANIA

Princeton Theological Monograph Series

Dikran Y. Hadidian

General Editor

44

CALVIN'S DOXOLOGY
Worship in the 1559 *Institutes* with a View to
Contemporary Worship Renewal

Copyright © 1997 by Pamela Ann Moeller

Published by

Pickwick Publications
4137 Timberlane Drive
Allison Park, PA 15101-2932
USA

Printed on Acid Free Paper in the United States of America

Library of Congress Cataloging-in-Publication Data

Moeller, Pamela Ann, 1947-
    Calvin's doxology : worship in the 1559 Institutes with a view
to contemporary worship renewal / Pamela Ann Moeller.
        p.   cm. -- (Princeton theological monograph series ; 44)
    Includes bibliographical references and index.
    ISBN 1-55635-035-X
    1. Calvin, Jean, 1509-1564. Institutio Christianae religionis.
    2. Calvin, Jean, 1509-1564--Contributions in concept of worship.
    3. God--Worship and love--History of doctrines--16th century.
    4. Worship--History of doctrines--16th century.   I. Title.
    II. Series.
    BX9420.I69M64   1997
    264'.042--dc21   97-39259
                                                              CIP

CONTENTS

PREFACE

  Calvin's view of worship as addressed in the 1559 *Institutes* cannot be discovered by reading any particular section of that *opus*. Rather, throughout the *Institutes*, in the midst of discourses on theology, ecclesiology, or the law, we discover Calvin talking about worship. Calvin permits no separation of any of the concerns of Christian life from worship, nor will he allow public worship to be separated from private worship.

  Calvin makes strong claims about the preaching of gospel and the celebration of sacraments being primarily God's gracious gifts to us. His claim that our response only begins in public worship and is most fully expressed in daily living is not quite so explicit, though equally strong. Nevertheless, Calvin cannot make absolute distinctions between these two directions of worship. He sees worship as the sum of Christian life—in other words, true Christian life is worship. God constitutes worship by accommodating the divine self—in giving the law, scripture, Jesus of Nazareth, the church, preaching, the sacraments, prayer, the Spirit, faith—to the very basics of corporeal being, so that human creatures will be assured of God's gracious love toward them and hunger to be in intimate relationship with them. God's gifts are not things, but essentials of relationship. Therefore worship also includes human response as the whole human life is expressive of discourse with God. Consequently, most of our worship takes place outside the sanctuary doors and in regard to other human beings. Life in loving relationship with God means life in loving relationship with others.

  This view of worship provides some useful insights for consideration of worship in any era. If one accepts Calvin's larger view, one sees that worship is intended to be dialogical, heartfelt, whole-person engaging, personal, corporate, accommodating, honest, bound to the fundamental claim of gospel, enlarging of God's graciousness. Calvin does, of course, make some specific claims which contradict this larger view. Yet his bottom line is always that worship offers Christ—not as eternal truth or doctrine or theological premise, but as life-giving loving relationship with God and humankind.

Many have helped move this work along. Don Saliers and Catherine Gonzales were particularly helpful in its early stages. Fred Craddock encouraged me toward publication by including it in his bibliography for his graduate students. Peter Wyatt offered helpful critique, as did John Hesselink. My own graduate students have strengthened my resolve to pursue publication by finding the work helpful in their own studies in worship, and hopefully many more will do so in the future. To all these, and to my most patient editor, Dikran Hadidian, I offer my deep gratitude for gospel bodied forth.

INTRODUCTION

The Current Situation

The latter decades of the twentieth century have produced a growing ecumenical convergence in matters liturgical and homiletic. This is evidenced, for example, by the BEM documents,[1] by the increasing agreement about normative patterns of eucharistic liturgy as expressive of our thanksgiving, by the move of "mainline" denominations toward a theology and practice of baptism as a rite of initiation, by the growing recognition of scripturally grounded preaching as an essential, but not the only essential, part of corporate worship. We recognize many benefits of productive research in the fields of liturgiology, biblical scholarship, and historical theology, particularly in the New Testament and patristic eras. We are increasingly aware of the historical interplay between the development of the church and the development of the canon, between the development of worship patterns and the development of theology, and between sacraments and proclamation of the Word. Moreover, we face increasingly empty pews in many denominations, while the phenomenon of "Seeker" communities challenges us to come up with worship events that truly address contemporary people's needs and realities.

We struggle to clarify values and guidelines for authentic worship, values and guidelines informed by matters of scholarship as well as faith, by scripture as well as by contemporary experience. Some hunger for the earliest, most pure forms of worship, lured, perhaps, by the idea that the prayers and worship patterns closest to Jesus must certainly be the most authentically Christian and thus significantly determinative of our worship.[2] As well, given a world that expresses itself fully as religiously pluralistic, we may indeed find ourselves more closely related to the earliest Christians than to any other historical group.

The Reformers as Valuable Resources?

It is easy for those seeking a pristine paradigm of worship to consider that the theological efforts of the Reformers in the arena of worship are at this juncture of little further use. Others, seemingly quite happy to throw out every shred of worship heritage, will likely be even less interested in what the Luthers, Calvins and Zwinglis might have to say about worship. From a contemporary perspective, it is reasonable to consider that the Reformers worked under severe handicaps. In the first place, they were only 400 years closer to the *chronos* of Jesus than we are. Yet they had considerably less access to much of the early literature many now consider to be critical to contemporary understanding of what worship should be and do. Secondly, our range of critical methods of biblical study was not available to bridge the gap in time and space, either to be applied to scripture or to liturgical or homiletic texts. Third, Luther, Calvin and others operated in a polemical framework that unquestionably shaped theology and patterns of worship, a polemical spirit that seems diametrically opposed to our own awareness of the value of and struggle towards ecumenism. Fourth, no one can deny that the Reformers inherited certain medieval ideas which influenced their theological thought and their worship patterns in ways that seem to us to be excessive. Witness, for example, the penitentialism in Calvin's *Form of Church Prayers*,[3] a penitentialism we find excessive and somehow inappropriate in our contemporary world. Fifth, the Reformers could assume Christendom. We live in an environment where not only does Christianity represent a minority within a largely accepted religious pluralism, but increasingly people seek out a Christian experience outside of traditional patterns.

Dramatically distanced, then, from the primitive church, and also from us, the Reformers seem to suffer under handicaps sufficient to render highly suspect any possible contribution toward efforts to resolve contemporary worship issues.

Diversity in Worship History

Yet, if we take all our sources seriously, we can only admit that no singular, authoritative, definitive rite, prayer or worship pattern exists in them. We cannot in good faith attest to a single pattern of baptism in the New Testament (let alone in the later church) much beyond the proclamation of gospel followed by an event with water done in the Name.[4] The content of preaching changes, as early as the move from the preaching of Jesus about the economy of God to the preaching of the early church about Jesus. Even the use of scripture itself varies already in the New Testament, testifying to more than one pattern of interpretation/application. The several "narratives of institution" each reflects a liturgical theology and practice different from the others, leading my colleague, Stephen Farris, rightly to call them narratives of interpretation. We see the influence of pastoral issues on all of these, and geographic location, culture, and their related phenomena.[5] Polemical controversy permeates our early literature, and such dispute has always been a seed bed for the development of worship theology and patterns.[6] Finally, we see with abundant clarity that throughout the history of the church all these things change: prayers, actions, scriptural interpretation and use, language, frequency, interrelationships. Sometimes they change, we must presume, for theologically and pastorally sound reasons, and sometimes not. So, even while we may discern patterns within our worship heritage and accord them a normativity, when we examine the whole history of worship, we face a kaleidoscope of possibilities of content and patterns of interrelationship for our own worship. They are not endless possibilities, because we are vulnerable at all levels to the influences of our heritage, but more importantly, because we are ultimately bound by the good news of God's love for us as attested by the words and deeds of Jesus—an obedience that liberates. So our need for clarity about gospel-authenticated values and guidelines for worship intensifies.

If we have any sense of the history of Christian preaching and worship as reflecting an ongoing life in the Spirit, if we have any sense of God participating in and responding to human life through all its historical periods, we must assert the possibility that formative worship theology and practice may arise at any moment in time. Those who have settled so readily for the normativity of the third and fourth centuries, as well as those anxious for a truly contemporary worship, may yet do well to attend to those watershed years in which the life of the church changed dramatically, specifically, to the years of the sixteenth century continental Reformation.

Neglected Opportunities

I contend that we have given insufficient attention to this critical era in the life of the church, precisely with regard to the appropriation, generation and application of values and guidelines for worship.[7] Perhaps this neglect results from the seeming handicap of distance, knowledge and context that separates Reformation theologians and the earliest church. Perhaps our inattention has occurred because the nature of the Reformation church seems so unlike ours, because we are so anxious to heal the wounds of schism, or because we are anxious to worship fully in the present. I submit, however, that the handicaps under which the sixteenth century reformers labored do not disqualify them from providing significant insight into our own work in worship or from offering valuable ideas regarding the nature and construct of worship. Nor do such handicaps prevent them from critiquing effectively what it is we are doing or not doing as we struggle to know what authentic worship is and does on the eve of the next millennium. Indeed, in some cases it may be precisely these "handicaps" that are the source of rich ideas and insights into what we are doing and might do. If nothing else, Calvin's relationship to his situation and the seeming restrictions it generated for him in his effort to avoid misunderstandings *may* provide for us a mirror in which to recognize the shape of our responses to our own situation(s). More importantly, if we continue to attest that Calvin retains theological integrity, and certainly to the degree that we consider his work to be powered by the Spirit, then we have every cause to consider his work as a possible source of insight and instruction even in our very different time and place in God's history.

Calvin's Witness

Clearly, Calvin stands firmly in the tradition of seeking the *pristinam normam*, the purest, most authentic traditions in worship as aiding the establishment of guidelines for preaching and liturgy in Strasbourg and Geneva. Insofar as that is a significant value for us, we should find Calvin's thoughts of interest. At the same time, he strenuously affirms and attests the reality of the church ever reforming, and maintains a resistance against any one liturgical or homiletical pattern as right and good for all times and places. Calvin's commentaries and sermons reveal an ongoing and vigorous critical scriptural study, that, while not necessarily informed formally by all our current methods of criticism, certainly reflects the concerns treated by each approach. Nor was he a stranger to the need for compromise. The Genevan fathers did manage, after all, to temper Calvin's insistence on weekly celebration of communion. The fact that pastoral realities may redefine theological positions and worship patterns and inform preaching is a fact well known to and well attested by Calvin.[8] As to Calvin's ecumenical bent being destroyed by his polemical circumstances, he, like Augustine before him, was horrified at the rending of the church. He certainly aimed his efforts to recover the normacy of preaching and full sacramental celebration at restoring the church to its true self as the body of

Christ. Caivin adamantly attested to the reality of one body,
invisible though it may be, hidden, even, amid the most pe-
culiar rituals and behaviors. If we find Calvin's understanding of the nature of and intimacy between church and state
inappropriate or impossible in our global village, still we
must reckon with his total conviction that real Christian
worship is inseparable from the totality of life, and with a
worship pattern that reveals a clear move from God's address of us to our address of the world. To be baptized
means, for Calvin, hearing the word week after week, being
gifted by the supper whenever possible, *and also* living a
life that is one's *eucharistia*: giving of gifts of love to others in thanksgiving to God, both in the church and in society.

Consequently, I believe one can make a strong case
that a fresh reading of Calvin would support many of our
current worship concerns: the search for the most authentic
understanding and expression of proclamation and sacrament; the struggle to maintain the integrality of scripture,
preaching and the whole of worship; the effort to affirm the
inseparable relationship between corporate worship and
personal life; the desire for a worship pattern that truly
evangelizes (embraces with love both the faithful member
of the church and the seeker); the effort to define and clarify trustworthy theological values that will serve to empower and enhance our efforts to live with God in a manner
worthy of who God is and what God does and who we are
and do.

A Fresh Reading of the Institutes

The following chapters result from my study of Calvin's 1559 *Institutes of the Christian Religion*[9] in regard to
worship. I aim to reveal in Calvin's address of worship fundamental theological claims that can be of value to us in
considering what we are doing or might better do in our ongoing worship reformation to assure that it is truly faithful
to gospel.

A huge compendium of Calvin literature commends

itself to this work in addition to the 1559 *Institutes*: the earlier editions of that *opus*, Calvin's letters, tracts, commentaries and sermons, and massive secondary writings. I have focused, however, on the 1559 *Institutes* precisely because this *magnum opus* represents a lifetime of work that incorporates implicitly, if not explicitly, the inner workings of Calvin's mind and thoughts generated from years of exegeting, preaching, writing, teaching and worshiping. I make reference to other pieces of Calvin's writing when those sources provide a particularly vivid statement of the issue at hand or suggest an alternative view. It has not been my intent to prove any antecedent argument or support any particular point of view such as might be found in the secondary sources. Nor have I attempted an historical or developmental approach: my goal is rather a reading of the *Institutes* that will disclose a theological *gestalt* of content and process writ large.[10]

I believe such a holistic aim to be consistent with Calvin. The 1559 *Institutes* represents a theological whole that is certainly larger than the sum of its parts, given that Calvin does not merely lay matters out in a linear fashion, but integrates each theological concern with the others. Thus we find, for example, that worship is far from being a sub-category of Book IV's consideration of ecclesiology. On the contrary, Calvin addresses worship time and time again with reference to the human condition, the graciousness of God, the problem of election, Christ the mediator, and the nature of law and gospel. Indeed, we should not be surprised to find that when we read about the law, for example, we are really reading about worship. The difficulty, of course, is that one cannot discuss Calvin's understanding of worship apart from Calvin's anthropology, theology, Christology, pneumatology, ecclesiology, and eschatology.

This volume begins, therefore, not with worship *in se*, as Calvin sees it, but with fundamental theological ideas he sets forth in the *Institutes*, ideas that in themselves turn out to be both informed by and formative of Calvin's theology of worship. Only after surveying these basic ideas do

we go on to consider Calvin's view of worship as revealed
in the *Institutes*. What I intend here is a theologically inter-
pretive exegesis and expansive exposition. Because I have
wished to enable Calvin to speak to us out of his theological strengths, I have been less interested in making explicit
his theological limitations. Consequently, questions critical
of Calvin I may raise only in footnotes; more often, they lie
submerged in the exposition. Yet questions concerning the
limitations and inadequacies in Calvin's theology also enable the expansive interpretation of the resources Calvin provides.

Moving Towards the Future

The final chapter includes both an assessment of the
value of Calvin's basic claims about worship and a movement toward pursuing the implications of those claims for
contemporary worship. Because of the complexity of the
gestalt of worship, I have chosen not to develop a full scale
application of Calvin's basic themes to contemporary worship issues. I hope, however, that the values and insights
presented throughout this work will encourage the reader
toward, and be of significant help in, a critical consideration of the contemporary worship of the whole family of
God.

In short, what I offer here is a fresh reading of Calvin's *Institutes* that shows the depth and range of his conception of worship as the sum of Christian life, a life initiated and enabled solely by God, a life constituted by
dynamic, dialogical, loving relationship with God and all
humankind. My ultimate hope is that this work will have
the effect of enlarging God's graciousness to humankind
and our worship life both in sanctuary and in world.

NOTES

1. *Baptism, Eucharist and Ministry*, Faith and Order Paper No. 111, World Council of Churches, Geneva, 1982, and subsequent related works.

2. Curiously enough, this same kind of thinking does not seem to prevail in homiletic theory—or at least not in such an obvious way. It is not likely, for example, that any Protestant, at least, would preach patristic sermons—yet we consider seriously—and adapt, as per current worship resources, the so-called "Apostolic Tradition of Hippolytus."

3. *La Form Des Prières et Chantz Ecclesiastiques, Ioannis Calvini Opera Selecta*, 5 Vols. Petrus Barth, Guilelmus Niesel, and Dora Scheuner, eds. Monachii: Chr. Kaiser, 1926-1952; Vol. II, pp. 11ff. Bard Thompson, ed., "The Form of Church Prayers and Hymns with the Manner of Administering the Sacraments and Consecrating Marriage According to the Custom of the Ancient Church," in *Liturgies of the Western Church*, NY: World Publishing Company, 1960, pp.173-84. In this volume the *Opera Selecta* are cited only as OS, volume, page.

4. That is, the name of Jesus Christ, Acts 2.38, 10.48; the Lord Jesus, Acts 8.16, Acts 19.5; the Lord Jesus Christ, 1 Cor. 1.13, 6.11, or the Trinitarian appellation, Mt. 28.19.

5. For example, the word *baptizo* implies immersion. But what was done where sufficient water was unavailable? Or is this a metaphorical use of the word in the first place? Note, too, the later additions in *Didache*, for instance, that reflect pastoral exigencies. Later rites such as the old Spanish (Mozarabic) and the Gallican, to name but two, show clear geographic and cultural particularities as well.

6. We see distinctions between the early Jewish Christian theology and the Hellenistic theology, and can assume that liturgical practices were similarly distinctive. Tertullian disputes the baptizing of infants and the baptizing by women. Justin's First *Apology* and Augustine's struggle against the Donatists and Pelagians provide ample witness to the polemics of the patristic era. Melito's astonishing sermon reveals a violent polemic against Judaism and is a prime witness to the shaping of liturgical elements to counter theologically repugnant ideas.

7. Exceptions include Howard G. Hageman, *Pulpit and Table: Some Chapters in the History of Worship in the Reformed Churches*, Richmond: John Knox Press, 1962, and the work of Hughes Oliphant Old, particularly *Worship that Is Reformed According to Scripture. Guides to the Reformed Tradition*. Atlanta: John Knox Press, 1984. Both include a final chapter that focuses on implications for contemporary Reformed worship. See also Old's recent book, *Leading in Prayer: A Workbook for Worship*, Grand Rapids: Wm. B. Eerdmans Publishing Co., 1995.

8. See John W. Riggs, "Emerging Ecclesiology in Calvin's Baptismal Thought, 1536-1543." *Church History*, 64, #1, March 1995, and John W. Riggs, "The Development of Calvin's Baptismal Theology, 1536-1560" (Ph.D. diss., University of Notre Dame, 1986). Cf. Hughes Oliphant Old, *The Shaping of the Reformed Baptismal Rite in the Sixteenth Century*, Grand Rapids: Wm. B. Eerdmans Publishing Company, 1992.

9. John Calvin, *Institutes of the Christian Religion*. John T. McNeill, ed; F. L. Battles, Tr. (from the 1559 Latin Text edited by Peter Barth and Wilhelm Niesel [Ioannis Calvini, *Opera Selecta* Vol. III, IV, V. Munich: Chr. Kaiser, 1926-1952] including collations from earlier editions of that text and versions of the *Institutes*). The Library of Christian Classics, Vol XX and Xl, Philadelphia: The Westminster Press, 1960.

10. This risks reading Calvin out of context, i.e., not locating a particular claim in the midst of the particular controversy or situation in which the claim arose. Yet, Calvin, in collating his thoughts in the *Institutes*, has already taken this step. Thus we have the same hermeneutical choices here that we have with scripture, with the significant difference that the work comes from the hand of one person.

I

GOD'S HUNGER FOR DIALOGUE WITH HUMANKIND

Our very being is nothing but subsistence in the one God.[1]

The Framework of Relationship

Brian Gerrish has reflected that for Calvin the cosmos is not anthropocentric, but theocentric; that humanity has its place "as spectator and even agent of the manifestation of God's glory, in which alone the cosmos has its final meaning."[2] I think no one would argue that Calvin identifies God's glory as the ultimate value. Yet Calvin is also quite clear that the reality with which we have most to do is not monopolar but bipolar. Thus Calvin's fundamental interest as expressed in the *Institutes* lies not in the ultimate goal of the cosmos *per se*, but rather in the dynamic relationship between God and human persons as individuals and in community.

Calvin sets up this relationality in the first chapter of the *Institutes*, as the framework for the entire *corpus*. He is not content simply to define the extreme contrast between God and our kind, although he does accomplish that. No, Calvin's framework is a dialogue of polarities, the linkage of opposites, the warp and woof of a weave that reveals and centers on the interaction between that which is divine and that which is human. From the very beginning, then, Calvin inscribes the dynamic that he will support from scripture, theology and experience over and over again throughout the *opus*.[3]

Calvin explains that one cannot know the self without knowing God, nor know God without knowing the self. These two fundamental worlds of knowledge not only are so integrally bound together that we cannot have one without the other, we also cannot see which comes first.[4] But the chicken-or-egg question is not really at issue. What matters is the co-inherent knowledge, the existing dialogue without which human beings, certainly, have neither self-knowledge nor knowledge of God. Moreover, mere possession of this knowledge will not suffice. Calvin speaks rather of self-consciousness and conscious orientation, of being *in se* that is finally a matter of being-for-other. In short, the entire *summa* describes the matrix of God being *pro-nobis* and of humankind being *pro Deo*.

If we are to be who we are meant to be and live as we are meant to live, we must know that we are not born for ourselves. We are not complete in ourselves, we do not have ourselves as our motivation and aim. Human life's direction, motivation, identity is bound up in Another. The very purpose of human existence, says Calvin, is that we may come to know God. Humanity is "made for meditation upon the heavenly life."[5] This meditation has as its stimulus and goal not just knowledge about, but actual union with God.[6] If we attempt to think and do only for ourselves, personally or even corporately, apart from this link with God, we neither know who we are nor are who we are meant to be. Our identity is nothing, we inhabit the realm of defect,[7] indeed, we have no life.[8] Reverse the position, and the closer we come to our goal in life, the more we possess identity, true personhood, human being, and ultimate blessedness. To what other use, then, should we put our mind and will but the worship of God? What other path could we possibly want to follow but the one leading toward immortality? Where else will human beings find happiness?[9]

Self as Source of Knowledge

Here we have a first glance at the fundamental relationship: humankind is meant for God. Yet how are we to know this? We begin, as we must, with our experience of our very selves. When we look at our own being, we recognize the marvellous wonder of our bodies. From the hair on our heads to our toenails, from the texture of our skin to the inner thrumming of our hearts, we recognize the indisputable evidence that we have not made this extraordinary biosystem. We may think our own deeds are quite marvellous, yet even children, Calvin believes, can do nothing but admit human creatures are not capable of effecting such miracles on our own. Further, if we look beyond our immediate selves and consider nature, we must recognize that we cannot plumb its depths nor control it. While we may certainly damage and possibly even destroy nature, certainly we cannot recreate it. Calvin can only conclude from his observations that the entire cosmos, from the unfathomable reaches of the stars to the deep recesses of our own bodies, is a gift from some source beyond ourselves.[10] Who is that source? God alone fits the bill. How can we know that? Why, because

> ... in God's individual works—but especially in them as a whole—... God's powers are actually represented as in a painting. Thereby the whole of mankind is invited and attracted to recognition of him, and from this to true and complete happiness.[11]

Simply by attending to our senses in their inward and outward wanderings and reflections we must recognize wondrous God. The divine majesty is so obvious its manifestation can be "easily observed with the eyes and pointed out with the finger."[12]

Yet it is not only the marvellous things we see and experience that point us beyond ourselves to Another. For if we live amid stunning beauty, we also are surrounded by disastrous ruin and impoverishment. Try as we might, gen-

eration upon generation of human life has failed to rid the
earth of suffering. Indeed, humanity contains "a veritable
world of miseries."[13] Calvin will not permit writing off
these miseries as happenstance, for they, along with the
glorious aspects of creation, also reveal to us the truth of
our real condition. We often can neither prevent nor remedy endless human tragedies, not the least of which is
death.[14] When compared to the effort that was able to shape
the vividly and amazingly appointed and ordered cosmos,
human creative efforts at fixing, making or even stopping
are rendered rather limited, to say the least. Certainly next
to God's capacity to enliven human persons, our doings in
the face of death and destruction are but mere, illusive
shadows.

While Calvin readily admits humankind—that is,
the human soul—is created *imago Dei*,[15] he never wearies
of making note of our marginality: we are dull, stupid, slug-
gish, weak, ignorant and feeble, blind and quite incapable
of comprehending mysteries.[16] Unquestionably Calvin
wants us never to forget humility, for in remembering it, we
remember extraordinary God. Indeed, the worse we look,
the better God looks. Are we impoverished, inept? God is
Splendor, Aptitude. And vice versa: in the face of God's
grandeur, God's abilities, God's truth, we are revealed to be
utterly incapacitated.

God Pro-Nobis

Now it is one thing to recognize power, capacity,
splendor, truth, ultimacy; it is quite another to know that
wonder as God rather than some anonymous transcenden-
cy, or as a no longer interested or even hostile deity. The
one we are to recognize, Calvin constantly insists, is precisely God-*pro nobis*, God who is undeniably for us. This
awareness makes all the difference, says Calvin, since "ignorance of providence is the ultimate of all miseries; the
highest blessedness lies in the knowledge of it."[17] Still,
considering the mixed reviews on our reality, the witness

on the one hand of gloriousness and on the other of abject horror, how will we know God is really provident, actively provident, toward us?

God could indeed leave us to our own devices. But that would not be God *pro nobis*, and it is certainly not Calvin's experience. Calvin is convinced that God is indeed for us, at least as much, in fact far more, than we are for God. Yet Calvin's view does not limit God to God *pro nobis*, for Calvin strongly asserts that we have but a limited perception and do not know the whole of God. One venerable metaphor that Calvin favors in clarifying this concern is that God is like the sun.[18] As it shines on us and our environment, it provides us with the experience of warmth and light and thereby knowledge of itself. Still, we cannot touch the sun, grasp it in our hand, wander across it or fully understand how or why it does what it does. In the same way, God's benevolence "shines" on us, revealing something of the divine self, even while the immensity of God far exceeds the reach of our knowledge. There may well be an infinity of Godness outside our relationship. Indeed, God's "essence is incomprehensible; hence his divineness far escapes all human perception."[19] Calvin's assertion of this stands as a reminder of how "other" God is, perhaps even how alien, as well as how splendid. But he finally is not all that interested in the unknown of God, but in what we *do* know of God, which is of God-in-relation-with-us.[20]

Unlike the sun, God's providence toward us Calvin experiences as fully selfconscious and intentional. He supports this view of God by noting, for example, that creation exists for us to the degree that its treasures are not only to be used but enjoyed.[21] God therefore has expended the divine energy not only in regard for our need, but has gone beyond necessity to give us pleasure. Furthermore, God did not simply sit back to observe a finished creation but guides and sustains life with ongoing care. More particularly, the fact that we humans have been enriched and beautified superbly and profoundly reveals God to be not merely a beneficent deity, but a loving, attentive parent.[22]

This parental affection manifests itself further for Calvin in the fact that God does not function toward us only as disembodied spirit, ethereal intellect or bare physique. Even though the *imago Dei* finds it, home in the soul, for which the body is simply the container,[23] God attends to the holistic nature of the human species. God addresses the divine self with regard to every dimension of human being—physical as well as spiritual and intellectual. So God has crafted all of the cosmos to mirror Godself,— revealing the divine self not just in nature "out there," but in all of life, and most especially in the human being. Within our immediate environment, within our very own bodies we are meant to see, touch, smell, hear, intuit, comprehend, the footprints, voice prints, mind prints, aromas, shades and textures of the soul and heart of the divine. How could we doubt the graciousness of this God? And yet, "such is our stupidity that we grow increasingly dull toward so manifest testimonies, and they flow away without profiting us." [24]

Calvin demonstrates an amazing gift for propelling us toward despair. He exudes anxiety that we will become pride-filled and arrogant and thus shut ourselves off from the Wonder that is God-for-us. He dare not let us forget even for a second our precarious position. But neither does he intend to leave us sinking into the abyss. By naming our terrifying reality, Calvin sets the scene for an essential claim: God's kindness does not remain tucked safely within the realm of divinity, God actually accommodates the divine self, adjusts the divine self, to meet us where we are.

Divine Accommodation

This certainly is not a new notion. It is rooted in scripture, evident in the aim of rhetoric to render ideas in forms fitting the audience, found in the Fathers as they endeavored to explain scripture.[25] Calvin puts this notion to work similarly, making it function as well as the governing metaphor of the unique way God relates with humanity. Yes, our minds *are* too small, limited, dull to comprehend this Other for whom we exist and with whom we are meant to live in relationship. In order to aid us, God instills in all persons, without exception, "a certain understanding of his divine majesty."[26] Are we so marginal that we confuse the truth of God's identity with nature?[27] Rather than giving up on us and going on to find other things to do or making creatures with greater capacity, God plans to dispel our confusion by bringing us up to the level of the divine self.[28] Faced with our incapacity, our littleness, God lovingly responds with infinite capacity for us, God accommodates the divine self to our reality. Can we not see, for whatever reason, God in the world around us? No, well, we can look at our own bodies. Can we not see God in that with which we are most intimate? No, well, then God provides us with "a certain understanding." Are we still unable to put the pieces together? Well, then, God presents us with another aid: scripture.

The Gift of Scripture

Here we have a splendid resource, a veritable encyclopaedia about God. But scripture is not just about God, it is the divine Word, albeit in ordinary human language.[29] Such language provides us with a medium through which we are able to communicate with one another. Surely we should be able to understand God's Word now addressed to us in this way! Scripture, like spectacles, is meant to enable the eyes to see what somehow escapes us in the living portrait of the cosmos.[30] Moreover, scripture manifests God as "more intimately and also more vividly revealed,"[31] for God in person speaks in it.[32] What was hidden to us in amazing nature is now drawn out for us in particular speech. Yet not only does God "in person" speak, articulating the divine self in grammar and syntax, but God speaks personally. God, the ultimate rhetorician and the loving parent, addresses each reader or hearer at whatever level that individual has achieved. If we are verbal and intellectual infants, God coos and babytalks for us.[33] If we are young

scholars, the words and sentences entice us to the diction-
ary and grammar books. If we possess multiple degrees, we
are compelled to every source of knowledge at hand—
philosophy, the arts, science—to puzzle out the deepest
mysteries to be found in the written Word. As Calvin's own
works attest, he harbors no reluctance to draw on "secular"
resources to clarify the word.[34] Furthermore, scripture reveals how God's accommodation changes not only according to the ability of the individual, but according to the
times and situations. Calvin's address of the differences between the Old Testament doctrine and the New limns this
truth. The content of each testament is the same, but its
form changes according to capacity manifested in varying
contexts.[35]

With scripture provided us, we are to seek God nowhere else, for God always represents the divine self there.
There is no point in looking elsewhere for God now. Scripture is definitively, unquestionably the Word of God for us,
and it contains all we need to know about relationship with
God.[36] Even if we find it difficult, nonetheless, we do better "to limp along this path than to dash with all speed outside it."[37] Thus God again accommodates the divine self to
us, providing a remedy for our hopeless vulnerability to any
other source leading us astray.[38]

Certainly God is more than the written Word, more
than any combination of letters and any collection of pages.[39] There remains that depth and mystery as far beyond us
as are the distant reaches of the universe. God always will
be more than we are, more than we can grasp with hands,
mind, heart, no matter how clearly the divine self may be
revealed. That should, in Calvin's view, only encourage us,
precisely because we are so small. Perhaps, too, God
chooses to retain the mystery and depth to exercise us in
piety, as Calvin might say, and to entice us onward toward
glory.

One would think that we would embrace this gracious and splendid gift with open arms. But no, our condition is such that we find the gift insufficient. Our incapacity

continues to exceed God's accommodation. It is almost as
if the more grace abounds, the more helpless we become. Is
it that God's graciousness is ineffective? Words are, after
all, corruptible. They can be mis-pointed, mis-copied, mis-
read. Though words are signs (nothing but!)[40] that point to
the reality they offer, still such signs are not the same as the
thing they signify, because even the simplest signs can always be misunderstood. The very arguments that flowed
through the Reformation amply evidence just how slippery
scripture can be. Yet here we can identify linked bipolarity:
the *nature* of a God-given thing as valid, sufficient and
powerful in its own right as an act of God; and our *use*, or
appropriation of that thing. In Calvin's view, everything of
God is valid. What we do with it is another matter.[41] Objectively speaking, scripture suffices *in se* (just as nature
does). Precisely because it is grounded in God's being-in-
graciousness, in God's infinitely truthful identity, scripture
stands on its own as valid. Self-authenticating, scripture
needs no other support.[42] But on account of our severe limitations, we find scripture insufficient to convince us of
God's benevolence and of our dependence on God for our
very life.

Human Limitations and Human Sin

So the human situation is not really much improved
by our having been given scripture. In fact, it seems quite
the reverse. When we now look at God with the refraction
of scriptural lenses, we can no longer dispute that in comparison to God we not only lack capacity, we also lack purity.[43] If our obvious incapacity to equal God's creativity
left us with any pride intact on the presumption that our
work or intentions were at least good, we are now utterly
disabused of such a belief. Our bucket of pride irredeem-
ably bottoms out. Contrary to the illusive claim of the last
water-spot of dignity, corruption, depravity, and evil desires swamp us "from head to foot, so that no part is im-
mune from sin and all that proceeds from (us) is to be im-

puted to sin."[44] Dear Calvin does not stop there. We are
"puffed up and swollen with...pride,"[45] blind and "drunk
with self-love."[46] Our inherent longing for truth succumbs
to vanity.[47] We are so deluded and deranged that what we
do perceive, we pervert in our labyrinthine minds such that
"scarcely a single person has ever been found who did not
fashion for himself an idol or spectre in place of God."[48]
We are not merely idolatrous, our whole nature "is a perpetual factory of idols."[49] This perversity is not limited to
any humanly identifiable group—for example, the slow-of-
wit, the unimaginative, the undereducated, or even the obviously immoral. A "filthy mire of error" imprisons even
the most magnificent and distinguished of humanity.[50] Because of the Fall, we willfully head in the entirely wrong
direction, and so obviously evidence "foul ungratefulness"
in the face of all the wondrous gifts God has given us.[51]
Every human is downright disgusting, vile, abominable,
despicably unlovable. And what of the *imago Dei*?

> Therefore, even though we grant that God's im-
> age was not totally annihilated and destroyed in
> (Adam), yet it was so corrupted that whatever
> remains is frightful deformity.[52]

We can hardly miss the point by now that Calvin leaves no
room for even faint memory of self-confidence, let alone
pride.
　　The polarity describing God and humankind has to
do not only with capacity and incapacity. Since Eden, the
problem has expanded to become one of God's perfect
righteousness and our utter corruption, God's graciousness
over against creaturely rebellion, hatefulness, malicious-
ness. Add to our limited capacity our putrefaction, and the
insurmountability of the disparity is increased by geometric
progression. For Calvin, the fault rests solely in us.[53] By
our choice, we refuse to recognize who God is and who we
are, we turn our backs on what God so lovingly offers us,
and God does not receive any kind of desirable response to
divine graciousness and accommodation. God gives us

gifts; we abuse them. This results in a now unavoidable reality of our total estrangement from God. If misery accom-
panied us before, now we wallow in it: "how wretched it is
to be cut off from all fellowship with God."[54] It is wretched
because such alienation equals death,[55] for we certainly are
not who we are meant to be and therefore *are* not; our identity is nothingness. So poisoned, blinded, numb are we because of sin that we cannot now perceive in creation the
loving, merciful God. But herein lies a paradox: our
wretchedness is compounded to the degree where Calvin
believes it should "lead us by the hand to find (God)."[56]

From nothingness how shall we reach Infinity?
From incapacity, how shall we reach Capacity? From utter
corruption, how shall we reach Perfection? Surely we could
name no more hopeless cause. Can we do anything to
achieve our aim, personhood, life—union with God? Good
intentions will not suffice, for we are preoccupied with
malice and have no good intentions:

> For we know all too well by experience how of-
> ten we fall despite our good intention. Our rea-
> son is so overwhelmed by so many forms of de-
> ceptions, is subject to so many errors, dashes
> against so many obstacles, is caught in so many
> difficulties, that it is far from directing us
> aright.[57]

Good works will not suffice,[58] for where will good come
from out of the corrupt? "...Oil will sooner be pressed from
a stone than any good work from us," says Calvin.[59] What
then is left but abject misery, non-identity?[60] In short, while
we may be advanced in knowledge, we are hopeless left to
ourselves. While previous ignorance was hardly bliss, now
our only reality can be despair, for we are damned.[61]

Ultimate Graciousness

One would think by this time that God would be fed
up with this disaster called humanity, that God would respond with anger or abandonment. Not so. We are meant

for God, and God still plans to engage us in graced life with
the divine self. God's graciousness has already been expressed in creation and providence in the effort to make the
divine self accessible to us. We have been given the cosmos and the human being as a mirror in which to see God.
We have been blessed with the spectacles of scripture as a
remedy for our muddy vision, and scripture includes the
law by which we may direct our lives aright. Now God
grants what must surely be the ultimate divine graciousness, the accommodation *par excellence*: the incarnation. In
it, according to Calvin, our loving Parent, infinite God, becomes finite in Jesus Christ. In so doing, God "has accom-
modated himself to our little measure lest our minds be
overwhelmed by the immensity of his glory."[62]

Is it not enough for humankind to have God mirrored in nature, in the human person, in scripture? On the
one hand, it is not enough, because our perversity blinds us
to the truth that is surely clearly evident. On the other hand,
it is too much. Our capacity is so tiny that even if we could
for a moment see clearly through the filth obscuring our vision we would simply be overwhelmed by wonder. So on
both counts further accommodation is needed. Wonder of
wonders, God invests Godself yet again, quite in spite of,
and precisely because of, both our incapacity and our depravity.[63] Indeed, that our condition is our fault and not
God's or some "neutral" party's fault makes God's next
gracious accommodation all that more extraordinary to Calvin. God embodies the divine love in flesh and blood so
that the paradigmatic relationship between us and God shall
be lived out for us in the human frame:

> (The Mediator's) task was so to restore us to
> God's grace as to make of the children of men
> children of God; of the heirs of Gehenna, heirs
> of the Heavenly Kingdom. Who could have
> done this had not the selfsame Son of God be-
> come the Son of man and had not so taken what
> was ours as to impart what was his to us, and to
> make what was his by nature ours by grace?[64]

What was hidden in the marvel of the cosmos and shadowed in scripture Jesus Christ lived out in person. What was painted in picture and imagined in metaphor Jesus enlivened in flesh and blood: walking, talking, laughing, eating and drinking, weeping with humankind, comforting, healing and nurturing us. There can be no mistake here. For Calvin, encounter with the human Jesus of Nazareth constitutes encounter with God. Here in the words and deeds of Jesus of Nazareth God reveals the reality of God *pro nobis* definitively, concretely, relationally, interpersonally.[65] In Jesus, God intimately interweaves polar opposites into a tapestry quite unlike anything we would ever have imagined.

The God that one encounters in Jesus is indisputably the same utterly gracious, loving, accommodating God we have already seen addressing us in nature and in scripture. But God here moves beyond self-revelation, beyond imparting knowledge to an extraordinary and inconceivable measure. Now, in Christ, God freely chooses to declare us justified, forgiven, sanctifiable. Our penchant for resistance, rebellion, evil no longer stands out of the design of the tapestry. Finally we own the capacity for living in dialogical relationship with God, quite in spite of our weakness and abominable history of evil.[66] At last we can begin to see a new shape standing out in the weaving.

We have arrived at what for Calvin is the sum of all God's graciousness, the center toward which all things have moved and from which they move, the apex of accommodation. Christ is the essence of scripture, whom the Old Testament shadowed, whom the New Testament proclaims.[67] In Christ, the mediator between capacious God and incapacitated creature, between gracious God and hateful humanity, the two poles meet and definitively bind together for all time. But Christ does not simply *represent* this integration. Rather, "as soon as you become engrafted into Christ through faith, you are made a son of God, an heir of heaven, a partaker in righteousness, a possessor of life...."[68] Out of God's incredible love, united with Christ

we are declared lovable and loved and therefore embraced
across a gap we can in no way cross. Not only can God
cross it, God has done so, accommodating Godself to us,
meeting and being with us in our reality just as it is.[69]
    Calvin's favorite description of this embrace is
adoption, for in Christ we who were without identity and
utterly alienated from God are given the identity of God's
own children.[70] When one adopts, my mother has often told
me, one never knows what one will get and how it will all
turn out. While this may be equally true of any manner of
bringing a child into a family, a total ignorance of genetic
lines may well lead to heartbreak that could have been pre-
vented if knowledge had been available. Yet it seems to me
all the more extraordinary, then, that God should adopt us.
From Calvin's point of view, God surely did know exactly
what we were, and what we were was hardly a point in our
favor. If God had any common sense, we might well think,
God would have left us behind in the cosmic orphanage.
Yet according to Calvin, God chose to adopt us in spite of,
indeed perhaps because of the very hopelessness of our
case. Moreover, adoption itself only begins things. Following the signing of contracts comes all the work of raising
up to maturity the one adopted. Unquestionably, Calvin's
vision of humankind makes plain that we have an enor-
mous amount of growing up to do.

The Gift of Faith

    It does make sense, then, that God integrally con-
nects adoption with faith, which is yet another accommodation, another gift of God.[71] Faith is not simply intellectual
comprehension or even assent to scripture or creed. It is an
awareness of God *pro nobis*,

> a firm and certain knowledge of God's benevo-
> lence toward us, founded upon the truth of the
> freely given promise in Christ, both revealed to
> our minds and sealed upon our hearts through
> the Holy Spirit.[72]

Faith is so embedded in our being that we are deeply assured and confident of God's love for us. At the same time, faith functions as "a place to rest and plant your foot."[73] It is home, safety, respite. We cannot do without this gift, for by faith alone do we "lay hold on the mercy of God in Christ,"[74] come to fellowship with Christ, and thus to our true identity.[75]

      By faith we see the dialogue writ large. Are we ignorant? God teaches us.[76] Are we dull of vision or even blind? God illumines us[77] and gives us mirrors and spectacles. Are we reticent? God entices us, bends and forms us toward the divine self or, if we need stronger medicine, threatens us.[78] Are we lacking in obedience? God supplies what we lack.[79] Are we frightened? God relieves anguish and bids us address the divine self as parent so that we can know the source of peace.[80] Are we clotted with sin? God justifies us, delivers us, regenerates us.[81] Are we unworthy? Mercy is ours nonetheless.[82] Do we not know which way to turn? God leads us to Christ who is, in turn, the only way we can access God.[83] Are we ungrateful, unresponsive? God gives us faith and generates gratitude.[84] Are we corporeal? God gives us the divine self embodied in Jesus of Nazareth, provides us with human ministers and visible, touchable signs.[85] Are all our works evil? God gives us good ones, imputes worth to them, and accepts them as signs of obedience.[86] Do we not know how to pray or fear we will be unheard? God gives us the desire, promises to be accessible, and does not reject imperfect prayer.[87] Do we not know how to worship? God gives us the rules.[88] Is there any help that we need? God willingly gives it, and indeed, blesses us without wearying of the task.[89] In the face of all that, what more could we need, let alone desire?

Agent of Relationship

      Nevertheless, there is yet another gift: the Spirit. It is the Spirit who gathers all the elements together and

makes effective the essential connection between us and
God.

A major project of the Spirit is that of illumination.
In fact, while Calvin identifies faith as the instrumental
cause of salvation, he specifically equates faith with that illumination.[90] Without this illumination, this faith, this Spirit, there is no access to Christ[91] and therefore no access to
God. Without the Spirit we would not recognize God at
work in the words and deeds of Jesus,[92] and none of God's
gifts would be of any use. The Spirit transforms us so that
we can recognize and receive God's gifts, and gives us
faith so we can appropriate them and make use of them to
enhance our knowledge of God and self.[93]

As we know, this knowledge serves not for its own
sake, nor for our amusement. Its purpose is to turn our life
in the right direction. Even the turn is the work of the Spirit, as the Spirit empowers us to overcome obstacles like
pride and all kinds of adversity. Moreover, the Spirit binds
us to Christ[94] so that we may travel the road of sanctification, that daily surrender to God's will. In short, everything
that occurs in us as a positive response to God results from
the Spirit at work in us, rearranging us into conformity with
God.[95] Not only is every gracious thing in us the doing of
the Spirit, but Calvin boldly claims that God "does all
things through his Spirit."[96] If Jesus the Christ is the one *in
whom* all the polarities are bound together, the Spirit is the
agent which ultimately effects the bi-directional link and
makes the dialogical relationship of God *pro nobis* and us
pro Deo happen. Calvin clearly articulates a powerful Trinitarian relationship between God and humanity.[97]

Limitless Love

There are no limits to God's capacity to accommodate to us, to love and care for us, and there are no limits to
God's willingness to do all this.[98] Moreover, unfailingly
God acts first on our behalf. Our condition precludes the
possibility that it could be otherwise. But our condition

does not require this response of God. God's love for us alone causes God's being *pro nobis*. God's loving goodness constitutes the motivating factor in giving life, sustaining, redeeming, enriching it. This love is lavish and abundant. Its nature is always to find new modes of expressing itself to us, and it never fails us.[99]

There is nothing good, just, beautiful, lively within us that does not come from God. Nothing. Everywhere one turns in the *Institutes* one sees the pathetic state of humankind always and everywhere countered by God's incredible graciousness. It is all but overwhelming, this loving accommodation, this redress of our littleness, our frailty, our sin. The gifts of love and expressions of graciousness simply keep coming. The gracious accommodation *par excellence* is the incarnation, for here God puts into human form—the closest we can get to the divine kinship with humanity and therefore comprehensibility—what God has been saying and doing for generations. In Christ everything God has ever done or said *pro nobis* is found, and the polarities, the contrasts are forever and concretely intertwined.

One might claim that Calvin's constant address of humanity's wretched condition attests to our utter worthlessness. The glass is not merely half-empty, it is bone dry, dusty, cracked, chipped, and even holed at the bottom. Any sensible being would not hesitate a moment to put it out with the trash. But it seems to me that Calvin's God holds a different view. All God's constant, loving accommodation to us attests exactly to the worth of humanity. This misshapen, lopsided, cracked and leaky excuse for a drinking vessel is so precious to God that God engages in the process of turning it into the holy grail.

If this gracious, divine accommodation toward humanity is one part of the bipolarity, the weave spun out under the roof of graciousness and love, the other part is our response. With the event of Christ, our being *for God* is made possible and real. We are retrieved from the state of nothingness and restored to our proper identity. Our worthless works are imputed with righteousness, we are equipped to respond to God positively, to make something of our knowledge that we are for the God whom we know to be so liberally for us. Moreover, until we actively engage in this dialogue we are not yet ourselves, are not truly being.

Receiving the Gifts

How, then, shall we respond? There can be no question about what is appropriate and desired: We should "bestir ourselves to trust, invoke, praise, and love" God, we ought

> await the fullness of all good things from him alone and to trust completely that he will never leave us destitute of what we need for salvation, and to hang our hopes on none but him! We are therefore, also, to petition him for whatever we desire; and we are to recognize as a blessing from him and thankfully to acknowledge, every benefit that falls to our share. So, invited by the great sweetness of his beneficence and goodness, let us study to love and serve him with all our heart.[100]

Here we have abundant attestation of God *pro nobis* so that we may be *pro Deo*. Here we have clearly marked the dynamic relationship by virtue of potent polarities, but more importantly, by virtue of the linkages between them. There is God, and there is humankind. There is self-knowledge that leads to knowledge of God and knowledge of God that leads to self-knowledge. There is God's splendid capacity, and human limitation; there is God's purity and our depravity. There is our hostility, and God's incredible graciousness and love, and finally, our response, our piety. Here are the distinction, the disparity, the tension, the warp and woof. Here we see Calvin the rhetorician revealing God's endless efforts to bridge the gap. Yet we still struggle to participate in this incredible relationship. So there is more accommodation to come. The more is that all of this—the polarities, the accommodation, the gifts, the reception and use of them—is lived out in the particularity of the church's events of worship. For Calvin, Sunday morning (or whenever the community gathers for the same purpose) realizes all of God-*pro-nobis* so that we may be *pro Deo*.

NOTES

1. 1.1.1.
2. Brian A. Gerrish, "The Mirror of God's Goodness: A Key Metaphor in Calvin's View of Man," in *Readings in Calvin's Theology*, Donald K. McKim, ed. Grand Rapids: Baker Book House, 1984, p. 122. (Reprinted from *The Old Protestantism and the New*, Chicago: University of Chicago, 1982, p. 150-59, 345-51; Originally published in *Concordia Theological Quarterly* 45, July, 1981, p. 211-22). In his more recent work, Gerrish has noted that it is God's parental goodness that funds Calvin's doctrine of God. B.A. Gerrish, *Grace and Gratitude: The Eucharistic Theology of John Calvin*. Minneapolis: Fortress Press, 1993, p. 41.
3. 1.1.1-3, 1.10.2, 4.17.32. See W. Balke, "The Word of God and *Experientia* According to Calvin," in *Calvinus Ecclesiae Doctor*. Die Referate des Congrès International de Recherches Calviniennes. W. H. Neuser, ed. Uitgeversmaatschappij: J. H. Kok B .V., 1978. His premise is that experience is a fundamental operative in our dialogue with God, while scripture and Spirit retain their position as definitive. He claims, however, that experience is always *a postiori* rather than *a priori*—a difficult argument to sustain in Calvin or anywhere else.
4. 1.1.3
5. 1.15.6, 1.3.3, 1.5.1.
6. 1.15.6, 2.15.2, 3.25.2.
7. See Donald K. McKim, "John Calvin: A Theologian for an Age of Limits," in *Readings in Calvin's Theology*, p. 291-310. He addresses Ford Lewis Battles' *Calculus Fidei: Some Ruminations on the Structure of the Theology of John Calvin*. Grand Rapids: Calvin Theological Seminary, 1978. The latter is found also in *Calvinus Ecclesiae Doctor*. p. 85-110. Battles finds in Calvin a polar structure of extremes—with false positions reaching toward nothingness, and true ones toward infinity. The less we know of God the more false our self-knowledge is, and the closer we come to absolute negativity. The more we know of God the more we truly know ourselves and approach truth and infinity. Calvin says pointedly, "if you contemplate yourself, that is sure damnation," 3.2.24. See also 1.3.3.

8. 1.13.13.

9. 2.1.1, 2.15.4.

10. 1.1.1, 1.5.1ff. Calvin notes that even the philosophers recognized us as a "rare example of God's power, goodness, and wisdom..." 1.5.3.

11. 1.5.10.

12. 1.5.9

13. 1.1.1.

14. 4.17.8.

15. 1.15. Luke Anderson explores this concept in "The *Imago Dei* Theme in John Calvin and Bernard of Clairvaux," in *Calvinus Sacrae Scripturae Professor: Calvin as Confessor of Holy Scripture*. Wilhelm H. Neuser, ed. Grand Rapids: Wm. B. Eerdmans Publishing Company, 1994.

16. 1.5.11, 1.11.9, 1.13.1, 2.7.12, 1.17.13, 4.1.1, 4.17.1,7,32.

17. 1.17.11.

18. 1.1.2, 1.13.21.

19. 1.5.1, Calvin's discussions of double predestination reveal that he never fully appreciates the extent of God's graciousness.

20. Scripture reveals not God as such, but God-toward-us (*non quis sit apud se, sed qualis erga nos*, OS III, p. 86). Consequently, recognizing God "consists more in living experience than in vain and highflown speculation," 1.10.2, 1.2.2, 1.5.9, 3.2.6. This same notion is affirmed by Gerrish in *Grace and Gratitude*, p. 25.

21. 3.10.2.

22. 1.2.1, 1.5.3, 1.14.2, 22, 1.16.1ff, 3.20.38ff, 4.17.1.

23. 1.15.2, 3.

24. 1.3.1, 1.4.4, 1.5.1-4, 10,11.

25. 4.1.1, 2.6.4, 2.11.13, 2.16.2; Ford Lewis Battles, "God Was Accommodating Himself to Human Capacity," p. 21-42, in McKim, *Readings*. Reprinted from *Interpretation* 31, January, 1977, p. 19-38; Richard Robert Osmer, *A Teachable Spirit: Recovering the Teaching Office in the Church*. Louisville: Westminster/John Knox Press, 1990, p 113.

26. 1.3.1, 1.6.1.

27. 1.5.4, 1.5.12.

28. 4.17.15. Although this comes in reference to the Supper, it provides a splendid summary of the goal of God in our regard. See also 1.13.1.

29. 1.8.1, 1.11.1.

30. 1 6 1, 1.14.1.

31. 1.10.1. "Now we hear the same powers enumerated there that we have noted as shining in heaven and earth: kindness, goodness, mercy, justice, judgment, and truth," 1.10.2; see also 3.20.41.

32. 1.7.4, 1.7.5.

33. *Balbutire*, 1.13.1, OS III, p. 109; see also 2.11.13.

34. 2.2.16.
35. 2.11.13, 14.
36. 1.6.1f, 1.7.1f, 4.8.7,8, 4.19.9.
37. 1.6.3, citing Augustine.
38. 1.6.1-3, 1.13.21, 3.2.6, 3.2.41, 3.21.2, 4.1.1.
39. The controversy about precisely how Calvin views scripture
will probably never be resolved. Some resources are: Brian A. Gerrish,
"The Word of God and the Words of Scripture: Luther and Calvin on
Biblical Authority," in *The Old Protestantism and the New.* Chicago:
University of Chicago Press, 1982. Hans-Joachim Kraus, "Calvin's Exegetical Principles," in *Interpretation* 31, 1977. Tr. Keith Crim. Werner
Krusche, *Das Wirken des Heiligen Geistes nach Calvin.* Göttingen:
Vandenhoeck and Luprecht, 1957. Donald K. McKim, "Calvin's View
of Scripture." John McNeill, "The Significance of the Word of God for
Calvin," in *Church History*, Vol. 28, 1959. Richard Osmer, *A Teacha-
ble Spirit*, ch. 7. J. K. S. Reid, "Calvin on the Authority of Holy Scrip-
ture," in *The Authority of Scripture: A Study of the Reformation and
Post-Reformation Understanding of the Bible.* NY: Harper and Brothers. 1957. Jack B. Rogers and Donald K. McKim. *The Authority and
Interpretation of the Bible: An Historical Approach.* San Francisco:
Harper and Row, Publishers. 1979. Thomas Forsyth Torrance, *The Hermeneutics of John Calvin.* Edinburgh: Scottish Academic Press, 1988.
Wilhelm H. Neuser, "Calvins Verständnis der Heiligen Schrift." *Calvinus Sacrae Scripturae Professor: Calvin as Confessor of Holy Scripture.* Die Referate des Congrès International des Recherches Calviniennes Vom 20. Bis 23. August, 1990. Grand Rapids: William B.
Eerdmans Publishing Company, 1994. The same probability likely applies to other dimensions of Calvin's work, such as his understanding
of real presence, etc. See Gerrish, *Grace and Gratitude*, for a fine dem-
onstration of the complexities faced in sorting through Calvin's writings.
40. 4.14.26.
41. This is key to the defence against the perverted misunder-
standing of the notion of *ex opere operato*, that intended always to affirm the "stand-alone" validity of God's work. Most commonly, Calvin
will insist that we must appropriate God's being for us, in whatever accommodation, by faith. The validity of the gift is in its nature, our use
of it by faith will effect the desired results in us. I am indebted to John
W. Riggs for marking the importance of this distinction between nature
and use.
42. 1.7.2-5, 4.14.3.
43. When we look beyond ourselves to God, "what in us seems
perfection itself corresponds ill to the purity of God," 1.1.2. And, "what
is commonly reckoned righteousness is before God sheer iniquity; what
is adjudged uprightness, pollution; what is accounted glory, ignominy."
3.12.4.

44. 1.5.15, 2.1.9, 2.2.12, 2.3.2, 5, 3.3.12, 4.10.24.

45. 1.5.4. Pride is "as if a wall should say that it gave birth to a sunbeam that it received through a window," 3.12.8.

46. 2.7.6.

47. 2.2.12, 2.2.25.

48. 1.5.12.

49. 1.11.8.

50. 1.5.12-13, 2.2.18.

51. 1.5.4, 2.6.1.

52. 1.15.4. Too mild is Gerrish's claim that "without the recognition that their talents and distinctive constitution are divine gifts, humans are not—in the full sense—images of God." *Grace and Gratitude*, p. 44.

53. 1.5.15, 2.1.10, 3.23.8, 9.

54. 3.25.12. McNeill notes that for Calvin, hell is "*alienari ab omni Dei societate.*" *Institutes*, Vol. II, p. 1008, note 26.

55. 3.18.3.

56. 1.1.1.

57. 2.2.25, 26.

58. 3.14.7ff, 3.15.4.

59. 3.14.5, 13.

60. 2.2.25, 3.7.4; see also 4.17.41. Neither the Enlightenment nor psychiatry nor technology has succeeded in reversing the abject truth of the human condition as Calvin saw it. One need only remember the Civil War, the Holocaust, last night's news to be reconfirmed in this abysmal reality. See also Jürgen Moltmann, "Vicious Circles of Death," in *The Crucified God*, New York: Harper and Row, 1973. Tr. R. A. Wilson and John Bowden, *Der gekreuzigte Gott*, Munich: Christian Kaiser Verlag, 1973, p. 329ff.

61. 2.3.2, 2.6.1, 2.16.3, 3.14.10, 3.20.1, even infants are lost, 2.1.8, 4.15.10, 4.16.22.

62. 2.6.4, citing Irenaeus; and above.

63. We would have required a mediator even apart from the fall, so lowly are we, 2.12.1.

64. 2.12.2.

65. 1.2.1, 1.13.9, 24, 1.15.4, 2.6.4, 2.14.7. Calvin endorses the doctrine of the *Communicatio Idiomatum*, 2.14.1ff. But see Gerrish, *Grace and Gratitude*, p. 54, n.11, p.182, n. 78; and Joseph N. Tylenda, "Calvin's Understanding of the Communication of Properties," *Westminster Theological Journal* 38 (1975-76) p. 54-65.

66. 2.16.3, 3.11.2, 16, 22, 3.14.5

67. 1.9.3, 2.9.2, 2.10.4, 2.11.4, 23, 3.4.25, 3.20.21, 4.14.20.

68. 3.15.6, 3.15.5, 3.20.1, 4.15.6, 4.17.2, 4.

69. "...that nothing might stand in the way of his love toward us, God appointed Christ as a means of reconciling us to himself," 2.17.2, 3.11.1, 10.

70. 2.14.5, 3.1.3, 3.6.1, 3.11.6, 3.14.18, 3.20.36, 3.22.7, 3.24.5, 4.1.21, 4.15.14, 4.16.4, 31, 4.17.1, 4.18.19.
71. 3.2.35, 3.22.10.
72. 3.2.7. For a comprehensive address of Calvin's view of faith, see Victor A. Shepherd, *The Nature and Function of Faith in the Theology of John Calvin*, Macon: Mercer University Press, 1983.
73. 3.13.3, 3.2.14-16. One would think, then, that faith is totally firm and unshakable, 3.2.17. I fact, it needs constant shoring up, as we shall see below.
74. 3.17.1.
75. 3.15.6, 4.1.1. Faith is the instrumental cause of our salvation, 3.14.17, 21.
76. 2.5.10, 3.20.34, 3.24.1, 4.14.8; Christ is our teacher, 2.5.5, 3.20.48; the Spirit teaches,1.14.3, 2.2.20, 3.1.4, 3.20.5, 3.20.34; scripture teaches 1.14.6, and is the school of the Spirit, 3.21.3; sacraments are likened to tutors 4.14.6. for they "have been appointed to instruct us...," 4.18.19.
77. 2.5.5, 4.14.8, 4.16.19; Christ illumines 3.24.6, the Spirit illumines 3.24.2, 8.
78. 2.3.6, 2.4.7, 2.5.5, 10, 2.8.4, 3.3.21, 4.16.9.
79. 2.5.4, 9, 2.7.4, 3.14.11.
80. 1.17.11, 2.16.6, 3.20.12, 14, 36.
81. 2.1.6, 2.10.4, 2.16.1, 3, 3.3.9, 10, 3.11.1-4, 3.15.7, 4.14.14, 4.15.5, 12, 4.16.17.
82. 3.3.25, 3.20.14, (but see election, 3.24.17, and note "it is one thing to be offered, another to be received," 4.17.33. Further, the only "worthiness" required is unworthiness 4.17.42, and *La Form Des Prieres et Chantz Ecclesiastiques,* OS II, 12-18; Bard Thompson, p.173-84.
83. 2.16.3, 3.20.19, 20, 28, 4.8.7.
84. 1.17.7, 2.8.16, 3.20.3, 3.13.1, 4.17.43; faith is particularly the work of the Spirit, 3.1.4, 4.14.8.
85. 4.1.1, 4.1.5; scripture is a visual aid 1.6.1; sacraments are visible signs, 4.14.1, sacraments use earthly elements because we are earthly, 4.14.3.
86. 3.17.3, 5, 6, 8, 10, 15, 3.19.5. Works will not aid us toward justification but are acceptable after God has justified us.
87. 2.2.27, 3.20.13-16.
88. 2.8.1,17, 2.11.13, 4.10.8ff, 23, 27-30.
89. 1.16.1, 2.7.7, 3.20.2, 3, 44ff; 2.7.7, God's liberality is continuing 4.17.1.
90. 3.14.21.
91. 3.2.34.
92. 2.2.20, citing 1. Cor. 12.3.

93. "...that the Word may not beat your ears in vain, and that the sacraments may not strike your eyes in vain..." 4.14.10, 3.1.4, 3.2.33, 4.14.8.

94. 3.1.3, 3.2.35, 4.17.12.

95. "all the actions that arise from grace are wholly" the Spirit's, 2.5.15.

96. 2.5.5. Given our state, it may be most important to us that the Spirit is "the author of regeneration." 1.13.14.

97. Further address of the Trinitarian strength of Calvin's theology can be found in Philip Walker Butin, "Calvin, the Trinity, and the Divine-Human Relationship." Ph.D. Diss, Duke University, 1991.

98. 2.7.7. The singular exception for Calvin, of course, is the problem of the difficult doctrine of election. See Gerrish, *Grace and Gratitude*, p. 169f for a helpful perspective on this.

99. 3.20.36.

100. 1.14.22.

II

FAITH AND WORD

...it is by the faith in the gospel that Christ becomes ours and we are made partakers of the salvation and eternal blessedness brought by him.[1]

The Nature of Faith

We have noted Calvin's definition of faith as an assurance of God's graciousness toward us. This assurance suffices to give us a firm position in relationship with God amid our contrary realities. Without faith, we are capable of neither gratitude nor authentic obedience. Without faith life is meaningless, because only through faith can we grasp God's promises and embrace God's presence in our lives. Too, we have noted that for Calvin, faith comes to us as a gift.[2] We neither create it out of our own resources nor achieve it as payment or reward for our accomplishments. Faith comes to us solely out of the graciousness of God, attesting to that graciousness by faith's very existence in us. Yet unlike the inherent knowledge of God planted within every human being, faith is not something automatically given. Rather, God has bound faith to election, according to Calvin, and thus grants it on a limited basis.[3] So also God does not write faith into the genetic code of the "gifted ones," along with the capacity to reason, for example. Rather, God presents faith to us within our self-conscious lifetime. As is true with reason, however, God does not provide faith as a finished product. Like all God's gifts, it is perfect within itself, but in our use of it, faith requires nour-

ishment and strengthening that we may grow strong in the
life of obedience, gratitude and prayer.[4]

How, in Calvin's view, does the gift of faith nor-
mally become present to us? How is it made ours, and how
it is sustained so that we can truly live in relationship with
God? In the first place, Calvin says "faith is born from the
gospel."[5] He agrees with Paul that faith comes by hearing
the Word of God.[6] Still, Calvin will also admit, in discuss-
ing infant baptism, that the Spirit can and may bring faith
apart from hearing by working in the Spirit's own mysterious way within the inner being.[7] Yet the normal means of
instilling faith is precisely through the hearing of the Word.
Of course, for most, baptism actually precedes hearing the
Word. At issue again is dialogical relationship, and God's
graciousness as absolutely primary in that relationship.

We have already seen that for Calvin, God *always*
first approaches us in graciousness, and apart from that we
can do nothing to relate to God or neighbor effectively. To
the degree that we respond to God at all, whether by hearing followed by baptism, or by baptism that we later claim
for ourselves on account of hearing, our response is only
possible because God has first given it to us. Infant baptism
in particular stands as a stellar witness of this primacy of
God's graciousness. Such a baptism attests God's claim of
love for us before we are capable of doing anything to seek
it, let alone attempt to acquire it. For that reason, we may
reasonably consider the bath as witnessing faith's offering
to engage us, and hearing the Word as faith's ongoing opportunity to raise us up in itself. And yet, baptism only
comes to us because those who take responsibility for en-
acting our baptisms have already heard the Word and already stand in covenant relationship with God.

We are caught up once again in Calvin's intricate
weaving. However we look at it, the truth of the matter for
him is that baptism cannot be separated from Word. This is
not so because either one is inadequate *in se*, but because
the human creature is. Creaturely incapacity occasions the
abundant outpouring of God's graciousness. We need every

help we can get, and cannot "make do" with only some. To ignore one aid or claim it of lesser value, subjectively speaking, reveals disobedience born of pride. Calvin insists God's people must know that they have been given unique and particular carriers of God's gracious promises toward them so that they might have faith, assurance adequate to give them a posture of sufficient strength to maintain their part of the life-giving relationship with God amid all the madness of human existence. Key among these carriers are preaching, baptism, and the supper.

Yet we must recognize that for Calvin, the latter two attest to the Word, and that the existence of both bath and meal depends upon the Word coming first. "The Word of God must precede, to make a sacrament a sacrament."[8] This is so because the Word of God is for Calvin the foundation of faith, the source of the truth upon which faith is based:

> For by his Word, God rendered faith unambiguous forever, a faith that should be superior to all opinion. Finally, in order that truth might abide forever in the world with a continuing succession of teaching and survive through all ages, the same oracles he had given to the patriarchs, it was his pleasure to have recorded, as it were, on public tablets. With this intent the law was published, and the prophets afterward added as its interpreters.[9]

Scripture and Faith

Like the cosmos and the human person, Scripture "is like a mirror in which faith can contemplate God,"[10] or better, like spectacles upon the bridge of the human nose. These lenses serve as God's gracious remedy for the human incapacity and disinclination to see God in God's visible manifestations in the physical universe.[11] Yet scripture does more than merely sharpen our blurred vision. It directs our focus solely toward God,[12] illuminating our minds and hearts so that what we see we recognize, and to the level of

our capacity, understand. Scripture, then, funds doctrine,
for it tells us about God and God's will. Yet mere knowledge of God's will accounts for little. Certainly Adam and
Eve *knew* what God sought. They lost Eden not out of ignorance, but because they held the divine Word in contempt.[13]

The law certainly does reveal the content of God's
will for humankind, "but because our sluggishness is not
sufficiently aroused by precepts, promises are added in order, by a certain sweetness, to entice us to love the precepts."[14] One attracts more effectively with honey than
with vinegar. So we have here another example of God's
gracious accommodation to human limitations in the giving
of promises that are meant to entice us to and sustain us on
the difficult path of obedience. But is not actually experiencing the fulfillment of the promises of the law—
achieving the blessings of God[15]—dependent upon human
works? Alas, we are quite incapable of any such accomplishment. But God's love for us will not, it seems, be pre-
vented, and so there are other promises that "are dependent
solely upon God's mercy."[16] Calvin is emphatic about the
nature of promises, Old Testament or New: "any promise
whatsoever is a testimony of God's love toward us," and
these promises are always valid, precisely because of their
nature.[17] Upon these faith is grounded:

> ...faith properly begins with the promise, rests
> in it, and ends in it. For in God faith seeks life; a
> life that is not found in commandments or dec-
> larations of penalties, but in the promise of mer-
> cy, and only in a freely given promise. For a
> conditional promise that sends us back to our
> own works does not promise life unless we dis-
> cern its presence in ourselves. Therefore, if we
> would not have our faith tremble and waver, we
> must buttress it with the promise of salvation,
> which is willingly and freely offered to us by
> the Lord in consideration of our misery rather
> than our deserts.[18]

We have assurance (faith) of the love of God for us. This

assurance, because it is not based on law and therefore on creaturely ability, can endure in spite of our limited capacity and the unavoidable failures resulting from the pervasiveness of sin.

Christ and Scripture

In Chapter One, we identified scripture as God's Word of embrace, God's gracious accommodation to human limitations, God's personal address to us in a language (human) that we are capable of comprehending, address inviting us to a relationship of life. We saw that Christ Jesus embodies that Word of love, such that encounter with the words and deeds of Jesus of Nazareth is encounter with the Words and Acts of gracious God. God's promise of mercy is revealed and expressed in Christ.[19] Calvin calls Christ the "substantial word,"[20] and the "Word endued with flesh."[21] The Word of God, Christ, is the essence of scripture.[22] Both Christ and scripture have their ultimate being and expression from God. In so far as both are the expressed Word (or speech) of God it can be said, as Calvin says of scripture itself, that they "flowed to us from the very mouth of God."[23] But because no one can now have access to Christ in the flesh, scripture "sets forth Christ as Mediator,"[24] both in the Old Testament and in the New. The Old Testament has the same foundation as the new: Christ. But only by image and shadow does it reveal Christ and serve as an introduction to the hope of the gospel. Its covenant is the same covenant that Christ fulfills and ratifies, but it is especially the New Testament that "reveals the very substance of truth as present."[25] So Calvin can say that Christ is everything that is worth knowing, for Christ is salvation.[26]

Gospel "clothes" and "offers" Christ and all Christ's benefits.[27] "Gospel" includes, in a general way, all of scripture as attestation to Christ, but Gospel is most particularly "the proclamation of the grace manifested in Christ."[28] In this proclamation we are offered not just the shadows and figures of the law, but "a present fullness of spiritual benefits"[29] that is ours as we have Christ within us through faith in God's promises. Yet again, the "sum of the gospel is held to consist in repentance and forgiveness of sins."[30] Both benefits become ours when in faith we recognize who Christ is and receive Christ in faith. So Scripture is not just words *about* the Word, it actually contains gospel, the essence of which is Christ. We deal with real presence here, presence as substantive and dynamic as that experienced by those who touched and were touched by Jesus of Nazareth.[31] Moreover, "the sum of the gospel embassy is to reconcile us to God, since God is willing to receive us into grace through Christ, not counting our sins against us."[32] In other words, Christ not only fulfills the law for us, thus sparing us God's wrath and condemnation. Christ also fulfills the promises so that we, God's children adopted in Christ, truly experience the fulfillment of the promises.[33] Through scripture, by faith, we are united to Christ and thus put into proper relationship with God, and are given the life that makes a human being truly human. For Calvin, gospel is not merely an idea, nor cognitive truth, nor knowledge, but relationship.

A Present Reality

At the very least, that means that Calvin also affirms a partially realized eschatology.[34] While we come to own the complete life with God only "in heaven," even now we benefit from God's love, else how could there be Christ?[35] That is, if we do not now benefit, then Jesus of Nazareth was not the Christ. If he was, then we must even now benefit from that reality. The very existence of scripture, faith, and the church verify the fact that our transforming relationship with God is underway. Our sins are forgiven now, not sometime in the future. Calvin says that as soon as people are, "by knowledge of the gospel and illumination of the Holy Spirit, called into the fellowship of Christ, eternal life begins in them."[36] In order that we might persevere in faith in spite of contrary inclinations and events, Christ gives us *now* all things necessary:

> Now he arms and equips us with his power, adorns us with his beauty and magnificence, enriches us with his wealth. These benefits, then, give us the most fruitful occasion to glory, and also provide us with confidence to struggle fearlessly against the devil, sin, and death. Finally, clothed with his righteousness, we can valiantly rise above all the world's reproaches; and just as he himself lavishes his gifts upon us, so may we, in return, bring forth fruit to his glory.[37]

This "already but not yet" reality harmonizes readily with Calvin's understanding of the dialogical, relational existence that we live with God while we remain in the world. Yes, the benefits are spiritual, but they are nonetheless real. This is further borne out by Calvin's belief that subjectively speaking, faith is not only something we have but something we do, since it is inseparable from obedience. We could not act out faith without benefiting here and now from Christ's gains. Yes, because sin remains ever with us, we do not always keep faith. But God never fails to be faithful, and constantly and graciously offers love to corporeal, limited creatures.[38] As we are empowered by God's graciousness, we respond faithfully, that is, with gratitude and the obedience of love.

The Work of the Spirit

That scripture proclaims, clothes, and even offers Christ, attests that scripture *in se* is not identical with the Word of God, that is Christ. How then can anyone call scripture the Word of God?[39] The Word of God is "contained" there, and we are to look nowhere else for God's Word.[40] Scripture is the Word of God—direct address in which we experience not only God's existence but also God's benevolent, gracious will toward us—*when we embrace Christ*. But this is so not in scripture's state of paper

and ink, nor in letter, but in the Spirit, when the Spirit en-
livens it. At the same time, there is an "indissoluble bond"
between scripture and the Spirit because the Spirit is the
Author of scripture.[41] So, believers are to receive scripture
as "having sprung from heaven, as if there the living words
of God were heard."[42] Consequently, the church cannot develop any new doctrines, arguing for them on the basis of
the free movement of the Spirit in the church. For the Spirit
cannot be other than what it is, and if God's truth is expressed in scripture, then the Spirit as author of scripture
must ever conform to that truth, to the divine self. That
does not mean, for Calvin, that scripture stifles the Spirit,
but that any work of the Spirit always coheres with the
truth of scripture.[43] Nor, as we shall see, does this mean
scripture does not call for interpretation. Indeed, the very
nature of accommodation, itself a divine hermeneutic of
many colors, shapes and sizes, implies scripture also admits
to multiple levels, metaphors, measures. Further, apart from
the work of the Spirit,

> the Word of God is like the sun, shining upon
> all those to whom it is proclaimed, but with no
> effect among the blind. Now, all of us are blind
> by nature in this respect. Accordingly, it cannot
> penetrate into our minds unless the Spirit, as the
> inner teacher, through his illumination makes
> entry for it.[44]

We may read all we wish, even memorize every
word from Genesis to Revelation. Nevertheless, without the
inner work of the Spirit, the reality of scripture and its
promises of gospel, indeed, Christ's self, remain objectively valid, but subjectively irrelevant. If humankind cannot
see God manifest in nature, nor, probably, in Jesus of Nazareth, why then should scripture be any different? On account of our human limitations and our corruption, we endlessly need God's accommodations to us.[45] So the Spirit
works twice in regard to scripture: in the generation of
scripture, and in its reception. In each case we again benefit
from God's gracious acts of accommodation to our needs.

Thus scripture is the Word of God *for us* in the process of offering Christ to hearts and minds being empowered by the Spirit to receive Christ. That is, when the text becomes a dynamic event between the Spirit and the reader or hearer, a lively conversation, a relational exchange, then Christ is offered *ex verbum*. Then the words become the Word for us, and we find ourselves engaged in relationship with God. So, while the casual reader of Calvin may be puzzled whether Calvin means Word/Christ or Word/scripture in any given case, in fact he means this: Christ the Word offered in the dynamic event of human encounter with scripture by means of the power and influence of the Spirit.

Thus scripture mediates faith, making faith possible by giving us the essential knowledge of the true God, by offering Christ to us, and also by serving as the medium by which the God dispenses the Spirit to us.[46] So also faith comes to us by the interaction of Word and Spirit within us.[47] Calvin speaks of the Spirit as "the fulfillment of the gospel"[48] in the same way as Christ fulfills the law and prophets, presumably because the Spirit binds us to Christ else Christ would not be effectively *for us*. This does not render either the gospel or Christ inadequate *in se* any more than Christ rendered the law and prophets inadequate *in se*. The truth (i.e. Christ) of the law, prophets, gospel stands valid objectively, period. But only by virtue of the Spirit do they have *subjective* validity and value, and become useful to us and in us. Scripture presents the Word, Christ, and the Spirit and so scripture "contains" everything we need to be God's faithful people.[49] But God *in se* is not contained there, nor is it with the book as object that we are concerned. There will be no adoration of the Bible in Calvin's churches, no gospel book processions, no kisses. The words on the pages and the book as a whole are but signs that point to God and that enable the divine-human conversation and relationship. It is no wonder, then, that without the working of the Spirit in us, there will be no faith with which we can grasp the Word. Yet because scripture empowers this relationship via the Spirit with whom scripture is inseparably bound, and because we cannot of ourselves either in our creatureliness nor in our sinfulness come to be in essential relationship with God, there is no possibility of Christian life without intimacy with scripture:[50]

> From this we readily understand that we ought zealously to apply ourselves both to read and to hearken to Scripture if indeed we want to receive any gain and benefit from the Spirit of God....[51]

Embracing the Promises

Still, knowledge of God and God's promises for us in Christ, while absolutely essential to the economy of our life with God, is not enough.[52] We must engage in a whole-hearted appropriating of God's embracing us in loving relationship and of that relationship being our only source of life:

> Here, indeed, is the chief hinge on which faith turns: that we do not regard the promises of mercy that God offers as true only outside ourselves, but not at all in us; rather that we make them ours by inwardly embracing them. Hence, at last is born that confidence which Paul elsewhere calls "peace."[53]

We must be by faith "engrafted" into Christ. We must become so united with Christ that we wear Christ's righteousness and are infused not just with the hope and assurance of promises fulfilled, but the *experiences* of promises fulfilled. Once more Calvin reminds us that gospel is not just an intellectual message, a notion, a sign of some distant future. Being in relationship with God in Christ is a whole-being reality, here and now.[54]

It will be no surprise that just as we cannot achieve faith on our own, even blessed with this gift of relationship we cannot of ourselves remain faithful. While we might hold scripture in the palm of our hand, embed it in the neural pathways of our brains, breathe the Spirit and move with Christ, none of us possesses the competence and ability to access faith completely, let alone preserve it strong and whole. Indeed, Calvin finds scripture to include numerous portions we are unable to grasp. He likens these to a bridle, by which "God keeps us within bounds, assigning to each his 'measure of faith' so that even the best teacher may be ready to learn."[55] Calvin might have done better to reflect once more on the transcendence of God here, rather than on the need to suppress human pride. Still, this view accords with his understanding of faith as a dynamism, a dialogue, a linkage of elements that expresses interaction, a being-in-relationship. We see this in the first place in the interdependence of Word, Spirit and faith given to us. Shut the door of hearing gospel and faith is cut off from its lifeline: "faith needs the Word as much as fruit needs the living root of a tree."[56] One does not need to be a gardener to recognize that without roots, not only does the fruit never grow, but the tree cannot come into existence in the first place. As roots are essential to the enterprise of being a tree, so also is the Word essential to the enterprise of being human. And it is an ongoing relationship: the roots do not exist and function only until the tree grows and bears fruit, but remain the essential undergirding and nutritional channel for the tree's lifetime. So also,

> we must be reminded that there is a permanent relationship between faith and the Word. (God) could not separate one from the other any more than we could separate the rays from the sun from which they come.[57]

The Human Condition

Our recurrent refrain reappears: this permanent relationship exists not because God's individual gifts are inadequate to their task. Rather, the human condition of weakness and dullness compounded by fickleness and perversity renders us in constant need of God's accommodation upon accommodation. Our faith forever requires an unflagging

support system. No matter that God's graciousness "is effi-
cacious of itself,"[58] no matter the constant outpouring of divine aids to God-given faith, our marginality is such that
we "are in perpetual conflict with (our) own unbelief."[59]
Given all the opportunities God offers us to experience the
divine self; given the dynamic nature of scripture as God's
own word, rooted in and manifesting Christ, permeated by
the Spirit that makes this Word available to us and thus
works faith in us, our faith ought to be solid as a rock.[60]
Objectively speaking—that is, in its inherent nature as
God's gift—it undoubtedly is so. But subjectively speaking, as we endeavor to embrace faith and to live it, we find
our grasp of it to be precarious and our expression of it fal-
tering at best. Alas,

> our heart especially inclines by its own natural
> instinct toward unbelief. Besides, this, there are
> innumerable and varied temptations that con-
> stantly assail us with great violence. But it is es-
> pecially our conscience itself that, weighed
> down by a mass of sins, now complains and
> groans, now accuses itself, now murmurs secret-
> ly, now breaks out in open tumult. And so,
> whether adversities reveal God's wrath, or the
> conscience finds in itself the proof and ground
> thereof, thence unbelief obtains weapons and
> devices to overthrow faith. Yet these are always
> directed to this objective: that, thinking God to
> be against us and hostile to us, we should not
> hope for any help from him, and should fear
> him as if he were our deadly enemy.[61]

Here is the worst thing. Daily all the hungers, anxie-
ties, despairs, abuses of human life confront us. As if that
were not enough, our disease is such that we not only think
God disinterested or non-existent, but actively, aggressively
opposed to us. It would almost seem better if we had been
left in ignorance, believing however wrongly in some other
God or presuming that God is uninvolved with or uncaring
about human life. But of course, as far as Calvin is concerned, this will simply not do. Humankind is meant for re-

lationship with God: not hostile, destructive-of-human-
being relationship, but loving relationship that alone gives
us life. So, in the face of doubt and all its attendant miseries, "faith arms and fortifies itself with" God's very
Word.[62] Assailed and assaulted from all sides, faith knows
the source of its help and flees to the Word lest faith evapo-
rate without this constant support. Nor can we ever only
aim to maintain the status quo by simply holding on to faith
once it is given. Not even the saints could survive without
unflagging recourse to the Word, for sin would ultimately
gobble them up.[63] Moreover, sanctification is precisely a
lifelong process of God's restoration of the chosen. This is
so because

> it never goes so well with human affairs that the
> filthiness of vices is shaken and washed away,
> and full integrity flowers and grows. But its
> fullness is delayed to the final coming of Christ
> when, as Paul teaches, "God will be all in all."[64]

We always face new challenges, and we grow and change
through the life-process of meeting those challenges. If
faith is to bear us up along the way, it must grow and become mature along with us, if not in advance of us.[65] Such
growth can only result from the constant address of the
Word to us, along with a repeated embrace of the promises
of the gospel, of Christ, at every stage of development and
in the face of every new circumstance. Christian life remains wholly bound up with scripture, so that with Calvin,
"may we not say that from the Word faith takes its beginning, increase, and perfection?"[66]

Dynamic Relationality

The rich textures of Calvin's intricate weaving continue to evidence polarities, tensions and linkages. Faith is
essential if we are to live in relationship with God, but we
cannot have faith unless God surrounds us with a garden of
divine promises. That God freely and gladly does. Faith is

the whole-being embrace of those promises such that we
can be absolutely assured of the truth of the promises.
Since we cannot acquire that assurance of ourselves, God
graciously comes to our rescue and gives it to us. Because
of our frailty and perversity we cannot grasp, maintain, develop or live out faith. So, with loving accommodation to
our reality, God provides for that need also, granting us in
the gift of the Word the Spirit who will work in us, feeding
our faith with ever new life-giving transfusions. The life-
lines of our relationship of faith are Word and Spirit. They
present to us again and again the essential content of the
promises of God, fulfilled for us in Christ. We embrace
Christ and the promises in the Word only through the work
of the Spirit, but we cannot have the Spirit apart from hearing the Word. Word and Spirit are inseparably bound, as
are Christ as Word and scripture as Word, and so are Word
and faith and faith and promise. There are distinctions, but
no singularities, no separations. One will not do in the place
of or in the absence of the other. Moreover, this dynamic,
moving relationship continues throughout our life, and it is
made perfect in us only in the eschaton, when we are finally wholly gathered into union with Christ and so with God.
The promises of and truth of loving relationship are real,
substantial, and present in Christ. We possess them through
Word and Spirit, but we do not fully possess them. So we
must constantly attend to the Word, seeking Christ there.
The Spirit constantly attends to us, opening us to the Word
and engrafting us to Christ. God's graciousness unfailingly
addresses our realities, as we struggle to be *pro Deo*.

Nevertheless, we must point out that Calvin does
not talk much of reading gospel, but of hearing it. The door
of salvation is opened to us when we receive gospel today
with our ears, even as death was then admitted by those
same windows when they were opened to Satan.[67] Yet
more important than this negative parallel reality is the fact
that we deal here with *relationship*, not data. We trade in
personal encounter, dialogue, engagement. And herein Calvin brings us to the necessity of preaching. It is precisely

the corporate event of preaching that makes accessible fundamental encounter with Christ Jesus, the Word of God for us.

NOTES

1. 4.1 1.
2. 3.2.33
3. 3.22.1ff, 3.23.13; Repentance is also a gift only to the elect 3.3.21, 24. Shepherd notes that "the most distressing feature of Calvin's understanding of election is that it is not an implication of his Christology; it is a surd." He goes on to say "While Pighius no doubt was a weaker theologian than Calvin, he was not weaker when he maintained that 'the whole human race is chosen in Christ, so that whoever should lay hold of him by faith may obtain salvation'." (*De Aet. Dei Praed.* 68). *The Nature and Function of Faith,* p. 95, 96. Gerrish, in *Grace and Gratitude* affirms that Calvin's eucharistic theology "is a better indication of Calvin's primary theme than is the double decree," p. 2. In agreement with these views, and because the doctrine of election is beyond the scope of this work, I do not address it here.
4. 3.2.19ff; 4.1.1, 4.14.8.
5. 3.20. 1.
6. 3.20.27, "…there is no faith until God illumines it by the testimony of his grace," 3.2.31. In 4.8.9 Calvin gets even more specific, saying that "faith depends on God's Word alone."
7. 4.16.17-20. In fact, "God works in his elect in two ways: within, through his Spirit; without, through his Word." 2.5.5.
8. 4.19.2, 4.15.2.
9. 1.6.2, "faith rests upon the Word of God as a foundation…" 4.14.6.
10. 3.2.6.
11. 1.6.1.
12. It "distinctly excludes and rejects all the gods of the heathen," 1.10.3.
13. 1.6.2, 1.13.21, 3.21.2, 4.8.9, 11.
14. 2.5.10, 3.2.16, 3.2.7; see also 2.7.12, where we note that it is precisely the promise of grace that makes the bitterness of the law palatable. So also 2.8.14. There are also threats, 2.8.4.
15. For example, mercy, peace, 2.6.3, and reconciliation, 2.7.2.
16. 3.11.17, 18.
17. 3.2.32.

18. 3.2.29. "...Scripture establishes this as the sum of our salvation, that he has abolished all enmities and received us into grace," 3.2.28.

19. 2.6.4, 3.2.7, 4.14.7.

20. 1.13.7. God's Word is Wisdom, the mandate of the second person of the trinity, who "is the express image of (God's) purpose. For just as in mankind speech is called the expression of the thoughts, so it is not inappropriate to apply this to God and say that he expresses himself to us by his Speech or Word." *The Gospel according to St. John* 1-10, Tr. T.H.L. Parker, *Calvin's Commentaries*, ed. D.W. Torrance and T.F. Torrance, Grand Rapids: Wm. B. Eerdmans Publishing Company, 1961, 1979, p.7. Following this (as also in 1.13.7ff) Calvin argues for the person of the Word as distinct from that of the first person of the trinity, but of the same divine essence. Parker also notes that Jesus-the-substantial-Word also speaks the Word of God. T.H.L. Parker, *John Calvin: A Biography*. Philadelphia: Westminster Press, 1975. p. 89. See also Gerrish, "The Word of God...." p. 66, and chapter 3, below.

21. 1.13.9.

22. Bowen notes that not all Scripture is essential for salvation, i.e., that Scripture is the container and Christ is the essential content, p. 71ff. Yet all scripture is essential for sanctification, p. 135. David Anderson Bowen, *John Calvin's Ecclesiological Adiaphorism: Distinguishing the Indifferent, the "Essential," and the "Important" in His Thought and Practice*. Ann Arbor: University Microfilms International, 1985. See also 3.21.3 and below, and see note 68, ch. 1.

23. 1.7.5. See our note in Chapter 1 regarding the various views of Calvin's doctrine of the inspiration of scripture, and below, regarding the work of the Spirit in regard to scripture.

24. 1.6.2, 4.14.7. "The Scriptures should be read with the aim of finding Christ in them." *The Gospel According to St. John*, 5:39, p. 139.

25. 2.10.4, 2.11.1ff, 4.

26. 2.15.2, 1.13.13.

27. 3.2.6, 3.5.5, 4.14.17, 4.17.5. Gospel is "the clear manifestation of the mystery of Christ," 2.9.2.

28. 2.9.2.

29. 2.9.3

30. 3.3.1, 4.11.1. So the "power of the keys" is bound to preaching, 4.11.1ff, 4.15.4.

31. 1.13.7, 3.2.6; Brian A. Gerrish, "John Calvin and the Reformed Doctrine of the Lord's Supper," *McCormick Quarterly*, Vol. 22, 1969, p. 88. Reprinted as "Gospel and Eucharist: John Calvin on the Lord's Supper," in *The Old Protestantism and the New*. Joseph N. Tylenda explores most carefully Calvin's reluctance to use the term "real," given the sixteenth century context. We would be more faithful to Calvin to use instead "true," he claims. Joseph N. Tylenda, "Calvin

and Christ's Presence in the Supper—True or Real," in *Articles on Calvin and Calvinism*, Vol. 10: *Ecclesiology: Sacraments and Deacons.* Richard C. Gamble, ed. NY: Garland Publishing, Inc. 1992.

32. 3.11.4.

33. 2.9.3, 2.15.4. "Christ was given to us by God's generosity, to be grasped and possessed by us in faith. By partaking of him we principally receive a double grace: namely, that being reconciled to God through Christ's blamelessness, we may have in heaven instead of a Judge a gracious Father; and secondly, that sanctified by Christ's Spirit we may cultivate blamelessness and purity of life," 3.11.1. Thus when Gerrish says that gospel "is, quite simply, the good news of adoption," *Grace and Gratitude*, p. 89, he understates the case (as the rest of his volume clearly attests!). Gospel is more than simply good news, it is the experience of relationship.

34. Parker has disagreed on the basis of Calvin's understanding of life as pilgrimage filled with afflictions, and of a present salvation in terms of forgiveness but not perfection or reward. T.H.L. Parker, *The Oracles of God: An introduction to the Preaching of John Calvin.* London: Lutterworth Press, 1947. 101-4.

35. 2.16.2.

36. 3.18.1; see also 2.9.3, Catechism, OS II, ¶ 270.

37. 2.15.4, 6. Calvin's address of sacrament (4.15, 4.16, 4.17) provides plentiful evidence of the present character of our benefits in Christ. We will address this in chapter 4.

38. Calvin notes that "the promises are never extinguished by our unfaithfulness and ingratitude," 3.2.32. Not only that, but God is known to "pursue miserable sinners with unwearied kindness, until he shatters their wickedness by imparting benefits and by recalling them to him with more than fatherly kindness!" 1.5.7.

39. 4.8.6. See note #39, Chapter 1, regarding views of Calvin's doctrine of the inspiration of scripture.

40. Catechism: "M: Where must we seek this Word? C: In the Holy Scriptures in which it is contained." (*In scripturis sanctis, quibus continetur*) OS II, ¶ 301. McNeill states "God's Word and the Bible are not convertible terms in Calvin's thinking...." p. 133; 4.8.8.

41. 1.9.1-3, 4.8.13. Co. I Cor. 1: 17, *Commentary on the Epistles of Paul the Apostle to the Corinthians,* Vol. 1, Tr. John J. Pringle. Grand Rapids: Wm. B. Eerdmans Pub. Co., 1948. p. 73.

42. 1.7.1. Note the little words, "as if." By these words Calvin refutes the possibility of allowing the physical text to become an object of idolatry. That idea is more strongly refuted by the fact that even if God's Word is located there, God *in se* is not. See also 1.7.5. Reid makes the point that Calvin's description of scripture as a mirror, which makes something visible but is not that which it reveals, affirms the distinction between scripture being the Word *in se* and in use, Reid, "Calvin on the Authority of Holy Scripture," p. 38.

43. 1.9.1, 2.

44. 3.2.34; 1.7.4, 5, 1.9.3, 3.2.33, 4.14.8, 10.

45. Augustine's long struggle toward true conversion until the curious garden revelation may provide Calvin's best example. Augustine, *Confessions*, Books 1-8.

46. 1.6.2-3, 1.9.3, 3.2.2.

47. 1.7.5, 3.1.4, 4.14.8.

48. 4.8.13.

49. 4.10.7, 8, 4.19.9.

50. McNeill, "Significance," p. 138; 3.2.33.

51. 1.9.2. Note that the sin against the Spirit is the deliberate rejection of the Word, 3.3.22, 23.

52. "For the Word of God is not received by faith if it flits about in the top of the brain, but when it takes root in the depth of the heart that it may be an invincible defense to withstand and drive off all the stratagems of temptation," 3.2.36. Parker notes that if faith were *solely* a matter of knowledge, Calvin's sermons would hardly contain so much exhortation! *Sermons on Isaiah's Prophecy of the Death and Passion of Christ*, T.H.L. Parker, Tr., ed. London: James Clarke & Co. LTD. 1956. p. 10.

53. 3.2.16.

54. 2.13.2, 3.2.35, 3.11.2, 3.13.4, 3.24.17. In addition, Calvin's discourse on sacraments emphasizes this same point, as we shall see below.

55. 3.2.4. See also Calvin's introduction to the 1560 French edition of the *Institutes,* included in Battles' Volume I of the 1559 text, p. 6.

56. 3.2.31.

57. 3.2.6.

58. 2.3.10.

59. 3.2.17.

60. 3.2.17.

61. 3.2.20.

62. 3.2.21.

63. 3.2.31, "Therefore, take away the Word and no faith will then remain." 3.2.6, 2.2.25, 3.3.10.

64. 3.20.42.

65. 4.14.8.

66. 4.14.11.

67. 2.1.4, crediting Bernard, emphasis mine; 4.16.19.

III

THE PREACHING OF GOSPEL

> *Since, however, in our ignorance and sloth (to which I add fickleness of disposition) we need outward helps to beget and increase faith within us, and advance it to its goal, God has also added these aids that he may provide for our weakness. And in order that the preaching of the gospel might flourish, he deposited this treasure in the church. He instituted "pastors and teachers" through whose lips he might teach his own; he furnished them with authority; finally, he omitted nothing that might make for holy agreement of faith and for right order.*[1]

The Necessity of Preaching

We have established that for Calvin it is imperative to know God in order to know ourselves. More, we must know God's gracious will toward us in order for us to be who we are meant to be: persons living lives of loving, grateful relationship with God. Further, while nature expresses this knowledge, it is focused *for us* in scripture and particularly in the promises of the gospel, promises which Christ Jesus concretely realizes. Faith rests on these promises, faith as utter assurance that God loves us and claims us for lively, loving relationship with the divine self; assurance that frees us to relinquish any other claim and depend solely on God for our true life. This faith comes to us as a gift, the reception and use of which depends upon the working of the Spirit.

Because we are who we are, both limited and devas-

tated by sin, we must hear again and again of God, of
God's sympathy and love for us, of the promises, of Christ.
Our faith, once begun, needs constant nourishment and support, or else like the body deprived of bread and water, our
faith wastes away to nothingness. We must hear the Word,
gospel, the promises over and over in the context of each
new day, each reality we address. We must learn ever anew
and in depth of this gracious God, who meets our need at
every turn no matter our poverty, rebellion, fear or despair.
Precisely because we are human, we must ever have sure
and close access to this knowledge, these promises, Christ,
who is God-in-relationship with us. What relationship can
survive without expressions of love and appreciation between the partners? So, for our sake, God has focussed access to the promises, to encounter with gracious God, in the
church's preaching.

    If we think we can perceive God in nature by our-
selves, we are full of folly and pride, for it was in recognition of our inability to correctly do so that God gave us
scripture. So also, if we think we can recognize and embrace God's Word and will for us there on our own, we are
equally foolish. Even aided by the Spirit, at every turn we
encounter ideas, terms and contexts so alien to us that the
very text we read convinces us of our astonishing ignorance
and incompetence at comprehending what is of God for us.[2]
And because of our perversity, any isolated, incapacitated
address of scripture is as likely to set us on the path to perdition and idolatry as not.[3] To spare us, and help us to come
and remain safely in relationship with the divine Self, God
gives us preaching, the Word of God come to us in human
words, in human voices, embodied in the utterly familiar
and maximally knowable:

> (God) provides for our weakness in that he pre-
> fers to address us in human fashion through in-
> terpreters in order to draw us to himself rather
> than to thunder at us and drive us away.[4]

Like all God's gracious acts toward us, the preaching of

gospel is yet another of God's loving accommodations to the human need to be surrounded by and encountered through what we already know and understand by experience—this "ordinary manner of teaching."[5] Naturally God is not bound to this method of address, but we are. If scripture concentrates and focuses the knowledge of God-for-us, if the promises of gospel, more particularly, Christ, center and consolidate the graciousness of God *pro nobis*, if the promises are channeled into preaching and sacrament, and if these are found at the heart of the church, then we, in our confused, limited, uncertain state always know without doubt where to go to encounter our source of life.

The Church and Preaching

Thus the church serves as the fundamental locus for encountering Christ, gracious God *pro nobis*. Hearing gospel as part of living in dialogue with God is essentially singular and personal in that the Spirit works within each one individually. At the same time, this activity paradoxically occurs also as a fundamentally corporate event. We are assured of God's presence with us corporately,[6] in the gathering of two or three, for the church is the body of Christ[7] and the dwelling place of God.[8] This does not mean that God does not make the divine self present with us individually, but that we are *promised* God's presence with us when we gather in the name of Christ, and, as with all God's promises, this one cannot fail.

Calvin links his theology of preaching indissolubly with his ecclesiology, for the church becomes essential to our true life:

> For there is no other way to enter into life unless this mother conceive us in her womb, give us birth, nourish us at her breast, and lastly, unless she keep us under her care and guidance until, putting off mortal flesh, we become like the angels. Our weakness does not allow us to be dismissed from her school until we have been pupils all our lives. Furthermore, away

> from her bosom one cannot hope for any for-
> giveness of sins or any salvation....[9]

The church is the normative environment for our coming-
to-be and continuing-to-be in relationship with God.[10] That
means the church differs radically from a merely physical
residence for the Divine or a personal, spiritual retreat or
refueling stop. It is, rather, "'the pillar and foundation of
truth'. But what else do these words mean than that God's
truth is preserved in the church, that is, by the ministry of
preaching?"[11] God has entrusted the church with the
preaching of gospel, the encounter with Christ, the forgiveness of sins, indeed, the whole ministry of word, sacrament,[12] which alone allows for and nurtures our participation in the only real life which is life with God. Because
our perversity and incapacities are life-long, but more because our relationship with God is life-long, so also our relationship with the church must be life-long and constant.
We unfailingly need the gifts of God which are given to us
through the church, and we unfailingly need the relationship with the whole family of God in order to be who we
are.[13] Here we are nourished, here we learn how to care for
others so we can be well experienced in such ministry when
we go out into the streets, the workplace, and all our daily
affairs. This grounding of preaching, of the surest access to
the Word, to gospel, to Christ in the church means, then,
that our relationship with God is multidimensional. We
cannot be *pro Deo* apart from engagement with others.

Authentic Church

Which is this church? How shall we know it? Calvin speaks of the church as both invisible and visible. The
invisible church consists of those persons in all times and
places who, according to God's judgment, are effectually
joined with Christ.[14] The visible church can be found
among baptized Christians who assemble for worship. Yet
many such gatherings dot the global geography. How shall
we avoid being seduced away into one that is not the

church? Calvin tells us in no uncertain terms that

> Wherever we see the Word of God purely
> preached and heard, and the sacraments admin-
> istered according to Christ's institution, there, it
> is not to be doubted, a church of God exists.[15]

Such distinctions make it quite easy to determine where for
him the church is *not*: where there is no preaching at all,
where preaching is replaced by lies and God's Word is not
obeyed or cannot be found, or worse, where that Word is
"openly and with impunity trodden under foot."[16] Preaching
is essential since its offer of Christ via the collaboration of
the Spirit is the means by which the church is built up.[17]
Without preaching there will be no sacraments, no family
of God, no community of faith, no multivalent relationship,
and no life. If there is no church, how will God's children
be born and nourished in faith? How will they come to
know of the gracious God *pro nobis* and the life which is
ours *pro Deo*? Through the church God reveals the divine
self as *pro nobis*, that we might be *pro Deo*.[18]

Calvin alerts us that God has further eased our identification of the true church

> because he foresaw it to be of some value for us
> to know who were to be counted as his children,
> he has in this regard accommodated himself to
> our capacity. And since assurance of faith was
> not necessary, he substituted for it a certain
> charitable judgment whereby we recognize as
> members of the church those who, by confes-
> sion of faith, by example of life, and by partak-
> ing of the sacraments, profess the same God and
> Christ with us.[19]

Pertinent human actions aid us in identifying ecclesial authenticity. Nevertheless, the visible church in which the
true church is found need not and cannot be perfect. The
behavior of Christians, in spite of the participation identified here, is not explicitly included by Calvin as one of the
marks of the true church. After all, sin ever remains with

us, on the one hand, and one manifestation of sin is hypocrisy. We may safely assume hypocrisy will take shelter
within the gathered community.[20] The simple truth is that
the church is comprised of sinful, incapacitated human beings, wheat and chaff, as it were.[21] Nevertheless, we are
bound to it exactly as it is. Still, this does not have to be as
counter-productive as we might think. Even while sinners
permeate the church, the church retains sanctity. This holiness results not from the mistaken notion that anyone other
than Christ remains sinless, but from the fact that God con-
tinually forgives the sins of the faithful, regenerates the
elect, and chooses not to impute vestiges of sin. Christ engages in a daily spot removal of the church, attesting thereby that with even such regular attention, the church will
never be perfect on this side of the eschaton.[22] Perfection in
the church on *this* side of the eschaton is not possible, nor
its lack disastrous. Therefore, to cut ourselves off from the
church because of its hypocrisy or moral poverty equals
cutting off our nose to spite our face, since the church is
where we are to go to encounter God *pro nobis*. Alternately, were we to find a community of impeccably moral ap-
pearances, unless its worship life is up to snuff, we dare not
entrust our lives to it. So we are again thrown back on the
authenticity of preaching and sacramental celebration to
discern where we may safely entrust our lives. Therefore,
any church, "if it has the ministry of the Word and honors
it, if it has the administration of the sacraments, it deserves
without doubt to be held and considered a church."[23]

Authentic Preaching

Ah, but the world is filled with devilish minds. We
can readily see that the Word can be so obviously abused
not even the deaf could help notice. Human nature makes it
equally apparent that the Word can be subtly skewed and
poor, trusting folk be led down the path to perdition. Why
else does Calvin admonish all to beware of false prophets
and test everything against the standard of scripture?[24] Even
though Calvin will admit that absolute purity of doctrine is

not essential,[25] and that there are some doctrines of less importance than others that can perhaps tolerate a modicum of inaccuracy, he does not make it particularly easy for us to know in detail which doctrines are which, or what the limits of inaccuracy might be.[26] He seems to credit humankind with more than we deserve, for he apparently assumes we are able to tell clearly when essential doctrines are being shifted an eighth turn to the right.[27] But how, in fact, shall we know that the preaching we hear is authentic? Pure? That the Word is being honored? Surely we are dependent upon the Spirit, and yet were we not vulnerable to deceit, it seems quite possible that Calvin would not have had a Reformation in which to participate, and that he would not have had to expend so much ink in the effort to correct error and right doctrinal wrongs. How shall we be assured that the proclamations from the pulpit are what we so desperately need to feed our fragile and nebulous faith? How in our human vulnerability do we avoid falling prey to silvery but forked tongues?

We know from the preceding chapter that there *are* questions to be asked of preaching. Is this word from the pulpit grounded in scripture? Does this word bring us knowledge of God—not about who God is *in se*, but who God is *for us*? Does it engage us in conversation with God and one another so that we know ourselves to be helpless and hopeless apart from God's incredible love for us? Does this Word proclaim gospel, the promises of God for us as revealed in the words and deeds of Jesus of Nazareth? Does it show forth Christ as the one who makes possible our relationship with God, who gives us life? Does it effect that relationship, that life? Does it reveal that life with God is, paradoxically, a surrender of our worldly visions and hungers for a life of gratitude and love for God?

Right preaching, pure preaching, proclaims the Word of God, for God speaks in such preaching.[28] Our only source for preaching is, in Calvin's view, scripture. More particularly, right preaching proclaims gospel, the sum of Christ. It reveals that we are justified by grace, and calls us to repentance and faith.[29] Yet right preaching not only says, but does; it not only proclaims, but effects. In fact, right preaching does what scripture does: it "displays and unfolds" God's "power to save," and through it "God breathes faith into us."[30] Right preaching as the preaching of gospel offers Christ, and makes accessible all Christ's benefits.[31] Indeed, as Bryan Gerrish puts it: "In the proclaimed Word...we have the substantial Word, to whom the written words bear witness."[32] Thus in preaching we deal not with conversation about Christ, but the real, or true, presence of Christ.[33] Yet this is not the grace of substance, as if we could hold Christ in our hands as we hold scripture. Rather, true preaching offers the grace of substantial relationship with Christ who, as the one mediator and the treasure house of knowledge and wisdom, is what we need in order to live faithfully with God. Further, right preaching exposes us to the efforts of the Spirit, to righteousness and to the possibility and promise of living forever with God.[34] It offers and effects forgiveness, opening the door for salvation, leading to faith and sealing the grace of the gospel. Preaching generates life, sustains it by teaching and exhorting.[35] Such preaching rightly heard and obeyed cannot help but build up the church precisely because Christ is its source, content, and context, and because the Spirit is fully at work in it, working at making us one in Christ.[36] Do we not have the access the disciples had to the one who walked the roads of Palestine? Never mind. We have preaching, and in preaching that same Christ is present here, now, amid *our* gathering and in our geography, bringing us life, connecting us one to another to God.

Human Mediation

Then a new question confronts us. How can humankind, incapacitated creatures that we are, convey the Word of God, let alone offer Christ, particularly when we are so vulnerable to deceit and error, so accessible to the twistings and manipulations of our idolatrous minds? Is it not an utter absurdity, generated by the grossest pride, to consider that

we might preach God's Word? Would it not be more reasonable to consider preaching as a *response* to God's
Word? Would it not be better for God to speak to us directly so there would be no possibility of confusion and error
and idolatry? Not at all, for the Word of God is so powerful
that in unmediated address it would simply terrify us, deaf-
en us and "drive us away."[37] Yet in Calvin's view, we desperately need the Word brought to us, since without it we
have no faith, no hope, no life. We ought not to be surprised that God wills to use human teachers, for that is yet
another expression of God's accommodation to our crea-
turehood. Moreover, human teachers preach not a response,
not a perspective on, but the real thing: God's own Word,
because that is what we need.[38] Given Calvin's anxiety that
our pride will get the better of us, we ought not to be surprised that he sees this preaching also as an exercise in humility:

> (God) accustoms us to obey his Word, even
> though it be preached through men like us and
> sometimes even by those of lower worth than
> we. If he spoke from heaven...who would not be
> confounded at such boundless splendor? But
> when a puny man risen from the dust speaks in
> God's name, at this point we best evidence our
> piety and obedience toward God if we show
> ourselves teachable toward his minister, al-
> though he excels us in nothing.[39]

Calvin brooks neither refusal to listen to a puny or poor human preacher, nor any exaltation of preachers, either. Still,
Calvin will claim that "there is nothing more notable or
glorious in the church than the ministry of the gospel, since
it is the administration of the Spirit and of righteousness
and of eternal life."[40] Certainly it is not because human
preachers preach that we must attend to them, or because
they have any authority in their own right, but because God
is the author of preaching. God calls people to preach, and
God speaks through their human mouths and human
words.[41] Consequently, those who refuse to hear the Word

of God preached, who disdain the humanly bodied forth event of preaching, engage in sheer folly. Such attitude and behavior is akin to "blotting out the face of God"[42] and constitutes nothing other than a willful turn of one's back on Godself and God's offer of life. Such folk Calvin describes as "traitors and apostates."[43] But this is so only in so far as the preaching is indeed the Word of God, in so far as it is grounded in scripture and expounds scripture and proclaims the Word. Preachers are bound to this: "they are not to prate whatever they please, but are faithfully to report the commands of Him by whom they have been sent...."[44] One does not preach from the Geneva daily newspaper or from one's experience or imagination, but from scripture. Moreover, one's use of scripture must be faithful to scripture.[45] As we have already seen, everything that we require to live as God's faithful people is already contained in scripture. It is there where we must ultimately go for all wisdom. What could we invent that could possibly compare, indeed, do anything but lead us astray?

The Power of Preaching

We recall, also, the function of the Spirit with regard to scripture. In the same way that the Spirit empowers persons to perceive in the words of the text the Word of God, so also does the Spirit enable the hearer to encounter Christ the Word in the words of preaching.[46] Because preaching is grounded in scripture, and because the Spirit works to enable the preacher and the hearer to perceive the Word in scripture and sermon, preaching has real power. Because we are dealing with the very Word of God, it is not surprising that power is awesome:

> Here, then, is the sovereign power with which the pastors of the church, by whatever name they be called, ought to be endowed. That is that they may dare boldly to do all things by God's Word; may compel all worldly power, glory, wisdom, and exaltation to yield to and obey his majesty; supported by his power, may

> command all from the highest even to the last;
> may build up Christ's household and cast down
> Satan's; may feed the sheep and drive away the
> wolves; may instruct and exhort the teachable;
> may accuse, rebuke, and subdue the rebellious
> and stubborn; may bind and loose; finally, if
> need be, may launch thunderbolts and light-
> nings, but do all things in God's Word.[47]

And, if that did not say enough, citing Paul, Calvin later adds:

> "A power has been given us...to destroy strong-
> holds, to level every pinnacle that vaunts itself
> against the knowledge of God, to subjugate and
> take captive every thought to the obedience of
> Christ, being ready to punish every disobedi-
> ence." (1 Cor. 10:4-6.) As this is done by the
> preaching of the doctrine of Christ, so, in order
> that this doctrine may not be a laughingstock,
> those who profess themselves of the household
> of faith ought to be judged in accordance with
> what is taught.[48]

That being the case, surely nothing and no one could possibly withstand the rightly preached Word. Alas, we must yet reckon with predestination, that allows the preaching of the gospel to lead to hardness of heart. On the one hand, preaching is designed to generate faith. On the other, "that the Lord sends his Word to many whose blind-ness he intends to increase cannot indeed be called in ques-tion."[49] Yet this in itself attests to the power of the preached Word to do as God chooses. The preached Word is not too weak to compel the stubborn and corrupt. The fact that gos-pel, when it is preached, "irritates some, is spurned by oth-ers"[50] is for Calvin simply evidence that God has chosen some not to be persuaded by it. This is an interesting correl-ative of God's choice of speaking through human voice rather than directly with the divine voice. Also, as we have previously suggested, Calvin elsewhere understands the distinction between objective and subjective validity or ef-fectiveness. It is apparent that his convictions regarding the necessity of predestination prevent him from recognizing that here. Calvin does add one further word of wisdom: "I do not say that wherever the Word is preached there will be immediate fruit; but wherever it is received *and has a fixed abode*, it shows its effectiveness."[51] The Word rightly preached will be authenticated by Christian faith rightly lived. One must presume, of course, that God alone will finally judge that.

That preaching finds its ground and authority in scripture, and its power in the work of the Spirit, offers both a bane and a boon to preachers. On the one hand, because the preacher is chosen by God to preach, and to preach nothing but the Word of God, the preacher has the weighty responsibility to preach and to preach as well as possible, else stand in contempt of the Word.[52] Precisely because the preaching ministry is instituted by God for the sake of the upbuilding of the church, the preacher's address of and by scripture is not solely for the preacher's own edification. The preacher is accountable to God not only for the self but for the church, in general, and in particular. Failure to preach the Word to one's people constitutes violation of one's call, rebellion, apostasy.

On the other hand, while God chooses to be dependent upon human voices to make the divine voice audible, the efficacy of preaching does not finally rest with the preachers. In the first place, as we have seen, God is the source of anyone's ability and call to the ministry of preaching. God gives us the content, indeed, speaks through us, and it is the Spirit who makes hearing possible. So we have no excuse for pride in our preaching, because it is a miracle brought about by God through us.[53] We preach neither on our own authority nor on our own strength. Nor is God's choice of us rather than others predicated on some particular value or worth in us. We can be relieved then, to know that while right preaching is essential for the life of faith and for the life of the church, total purity of preaching is not.[54] If the words, ideas, rhetorical approach or even the moral life of the preacher slip sometimes outside the lines, because we are dealing with the truth of God, we can trust *that* instead of non-existent human perfection. After all, Calvin points out, as the honorable Augustine noted, hearers hear and follow the voice of Christ, not that of the minister.[55] Consequently, we can know that no one need fear to preach or hear preachers out of anxiety that one wrong word or sermon will utterly destroy an individual or despoil the church.

A Preacher's Tasks

Preachers do have their work cut out for them, hard work that calls at once all our attention and resources in concert with the empowerment by which we are graced by God. Failure to prepare thoroughly, even if one knows scripture as completely as Calvin certainly did, is wholly inappropriate:

> If I should enter the pulpit without deigning to glance at a book, and should frivolously think to myself, "Oh well, when I preach, God will give me enough to say," and come here without troubling to read or thinking what I ought to declare, and do not carefully consider how I must apply Holy Scripture to the edification of the people, then I should be an arrogant upstart.[56]

At the same time, preachers always know the source of their sermon and need never be in doubt about what they will preach: Christ. But this is not a generic Christ, a kind of whole gospel in every sermon content that can be written down once and repeated Sunday after Sunday in every church everywhere. For Calvin, each sermon manifests a specific interchange between the Christ presented in a particular text of scripture and the congregation in the pew. That certainly means that the first task of the preacher is the address of scripture, not the least part of which is surrender to scripture's address of oneself. This is the case because

> the Holy Spirit so inheres in His truth, which He expresses in Scripture, that only when its proper

> reverence and dignity are given to the Word
> does the Holy Spirit show forth His power.[57]

Obviously, the preacher's interaction with scripture is no casual, light-hearted event. Our approach to scripture must be equivalent to our approach to Christ the Word of God, and thus to Godself. Reverence, awe, humility and teachability are in order. There is no room for pride in this enterprise, only total surrender and dependence upon the Spirit both to make the words the Word for us, and to enable us to pursue the second task of the preacher: to address the Word in the words profitably to our people.[58]

Although preachers thus take notes in the school of Scripture, we are well reminded that Calvin believes scripture to be interpretable. It is not simply to be swallowed whole and verbatim. Scripture is God's accommodation to us, baby-talk in our faith's infancy, mysteries and truths "expressed largely in mean and lowly words."[59] Yet even if we can comprehend those words without help, scripture overflows with figures of speech such as metaphor, metonymy, synecdoche and typologies.[60] Scripture also holds within it complicated ideas that need careful examination if we are to understand aright and avoid muddying the Scriptural waters with contradictory explanations.[61] Then "what prevents us from explaining in clearer words those matters in Scripture which perplex and hinder our understanding...?" asks Calvin.[62] In fact, preachers must do this so God's people will know without confusion what they need to know to be who they are meant to be. Preachers do not only repeat what they have read in scripture. Preachers explain scripture, clarify it, paint a picture of it in order to make it come alive for and accessible to the hearers. This is the hermeneutical task of preachers, whom Calvin describes as "interpreters."[63]

Calvin's Exegetical Concerns

Of course, "we cannot understand the teaching of God unless we know what procedure, style and language he uses."[64] It is imperative, then, that preachers be first of all students of scripture as Calvin himself was.[65] We can easily see in Calvin's dialogue with scriptural accounts in the *Institutes* the well-trained scholar at work.[66] Reviewing the larger corpus of Calvin's work has brought Hans-Joachim Kraus to set out eight exegetical principles to which Calvin's works attest.[67]

1. Clarity and brevity.[68] The effort to clarify is evident everywhere, evidenced by Calvin's inclination toward enumerating points and summarizing.[69] Brevity, however, is clearly a relative term, and we can only wonder in comparison to what. Most commentary gives credence to the idea that the element of brevity is in service to how confusing the text seems or how badly it has been misinterpreted or used.

2. Concern for the intent of the author: "about the only business (the interpreter) has is to lay open the mind of the writer."[70] A regular testimony is the phrase, "as if (the author) had said...."[71]

3. Concern for the historical, geographical, and institutional setting and circumstances of the text. Calvin himself says, "There are many statements in Scripture the meaning of which depends upon their context."[72]

4. Concern for the "real meaning" (original, true, simple or grammatical meaning) of the text.[73] Calvin will have us know the literal reading, and critical to this is his consistent effort to know what the Hebrew or Greek words mean.[74]

5. Concern for the context and direction of the text,[75] that is, the relationship of a text to that which precedes and follows it.

6. Concern for the "living explanation." Calvin is never satisfied with simply noting what the words themselves mean, or even what the text meant when written. There is an elasticity to words, and some texts may be taken as embracing more than they say precisely. As Calvin says of the ten commandments,

> there are such manifold synecdoches that he
> who would confine his understanding of the law
> within the narrowness of the words deserves to
> be laughed at. Therefore, plainly a sober inter-
> pretation of the law goes beyond words; but just
> how far remains obscure unless some measure
> be set.[76]

Calvin's measure here is "to ponder why it was given to us,"[77] a measure that can be seen at work equally well in his address of Christ's prayer.[78] Beyond that, scripture is God's address to God's people now. Calvin readily reveals his perception of the contemporary applications in the words of antiquity, applications of the universal that underlie the particularity of a text.[79]

7. Concern for figures of speech. Under this term Calvin categorizes bread/body, wine/blood, since it would be "an intolerable blasphemy" to understand them literally.[80]

8. Concern to seek Christ. This comes as no surprise in view of Calvin's conviction that all scripture preaches Christ:

> This is what we should in short seek in the
> whole of Scripture: truly to know Jesus Christ,
> and the infinite riches that are comprised in him
> and are offered to us by him from God the Fa-
> ther. If one were to sift thoroughly the Law and
> the Prophets, he would not find a single word
> which would not draw and bring us to him. And
> for a fact, since all the treasures of wisdom and
> understanding are hidden in him, there is not the
> least question of having, or turning toward, an-
> other goal....Our minds ought to come to a halt
> at the point where we learn in Scripture to know
> Jesus Christ and him alone, so that we may be
> directly led by him to the Father who contains
> in himself all perfection.[81]

In addition to Kraus' principles, some other features are evidenced in Calvin's exegetical work. Even a cursory glimpse of any exegetically based text will reveal that Calvin takes little for granted, raising questions constantly. He does not take tradition at its word, either, but regularly and consistently places it next to the biblical word. Sometimes the tradition supports the word and the word the tradition. If not, Calvin gladly demonstrates how scripture undermines the tradition, often raging against the "heretics" of history past and present, particularly the Anabaptists and the papacy.[82] And while Calvin is not often thought of in terms of a vivid imagination, one does find evidence of such in his sometimes quite lively language.[83] Calvin does draw the line of imagination clearly, however. Allegories, for example, "ought not to go beyond the limits set by the rule of Scripture, let alone suffice as the foundation for any doctrines."[84] But we are not limited to the language of scripture:

> If they call a foreign word one that cannot be shown to stand written syllable by syllable in Scripture, they are indeed imposing upon us an unjust law which condemns all interpretation not patched together out of the fabric of Scripture. But if that is "foreign" which has been curiously devised and is superstitiously defended, which conduces more to contention than to edification, which is made use of either unseasonably or fruitlessly, which by its harshness offends pious ears, which detracts from the simplicity of God's Word—I wholeheartedly embrace their soberness.[85]

Calvin takes his exegetical responsibility seriously. He does not publish editions of the *Institutes* plus commentary after commentary simply in order to make available his opinion, but in text after text applies all his scholarly abilities and whatever resources are appropriate to the effort to make plain the meaning and import of the Biblical texts for the benefit of others.[86] Calvin punctuates his work with rhetorical questions. This practice not only exhibits his own method of addressing the text, but also of engaging his community. He is determined to enable others to experience real encounter with the word, and engagement with the Word of God. This intention, along with Calvin's exegetical work, underwrites all that he does, including his preaching. Because of the importance of preaching in Calvin's perception of worship, it is essential that we consider his own practice here, even if that takes us beyond the *Institutes*.

Calvin's Practice of Preaching

We do not know when Calvin began preaching—perhaps as early as the 1520s, but certainly during his initial ministry in Geneva. We have little information about Calvin's preaching prior to 1549, when Denis Raguenier began to take down Calvin's sermons for posterity. By that time, if not well before, Calvin's preaching pattern was well established. And we may safely assume that for years, if not from the beginning, Calvin has been preaching *lectio continua*, even though he does interrupt this process for major church festivals.[87]

We may take as a model Calvin's exegesis and sermon on John.[88] Calvin begins the commentary with an introduction that explains the meaning of the word "gospel" and distinguishes between John and the Synoptics. The same ideas shape the sermon introduction, but here they are at once simplified and expanded. When Calvin begins the commentary proper, he follows a method of dealing with the Biblical text phrase by phrase, setting out the meaning briefly or at length, depending on the character of the text. Calvin's sermon also deals with the text phrase by phrase, explaining as he goes, just as in the commentary. In the commentary he refutes the errors of the heretics: Servetus, the Arians and Sabellians, papal, Sophistic and Sorbonnic; and otherwise considers the tradition to date.[89] When he covers this material in the sermon, his references seem most often to be those contemporary to the experience of his people and more likely to be known by them.

In the commentary he deals with linguistic issues in a manner appropriate to that setting, noting distinctions between the Latin and the Greek.[90] If he raises such issues in the sermon, it is only because he could hardly explain the

text or issue clearly without doing so.[91] Detail is obviously
important to Calvin, but it must be used appropriately—that
is, with reference to the particular purpose of the task at
hand and to the capacities of his hearers.

In the sermon Calvin is clearly anxious that his people take his words home and put them to work in their
lives. As a result, a considerable amount of time and energy
is spent in the contemporary application. His pattern is to
repeat the phrase now being addressed, to explain what the
author intended by it, and then to make clear what its value
is for contemporary Christian life. This may result in either
a comment along the lines of "this is what we have to remember" or a more direct, but nonetheless gentle, exhortation. While such is not uncommon in Calvin's other works,
it finds its home in the sermon. Meanwhile, the exegetical
principles are not abandoned, for they have shaped the exegesis that shapes the sermon.

The same ideas that Calvin expresses in the commentary on John 1 are found in his sermon on the same
text. But there, much in the way that God has accommodat-
ed Godself to humankind and to our minimal capacities,
Calvin accommodates his words even more fully to his congregation.[92] Several things are exemplary, though they are
essentially a matter of degree, rather than novelty.

1. In the first place, in the sermon Calvin is less
terse and straight to the point. He seems disinclined to assume his people can fill in any gaps, let alone follow him in
quantum leaps from some specific concern of the text to
contemporary understanding. Thus he takes appropriate
short side trips perhaps unnecessary in the commentary, addressing *Paul's* use of the word gospel, for instance, and
whether John or Christ is the source of the Gospel *according* to John. This same pattern is quite evident in the *Institutes*, although there the side trips are often quite substantial.

2. While detail matters, it serves the essence. Calvin
will not tell his people all they might know about a text, but

only what will enable them to understand it. In the *Institutes*, Calvin is more thorough, though not as much, perhaps in the Commentaries. As with item 1 above, the particular nature of the *Institutes* as thematic exposition rather than *lectio continua* scriptural exposition will influence the difference in approach.

    3. Calvin uses the tool of rhetoric as he sees fit. Hardly ignorant of the classical tradition,[93] Calvin nonetheless submits the discipline to scripture, which has a rhetoric all its own. His *lectio continua* preaching style commits him to following the order of the text rather than the logical order of argument expected in classic rhetoric.[94] He is naturally freer to pursue the traditional pattern in the *Institutes*. And as regards language, while he affirms the arts as the gift of the Spirit to have their place, undue eloquence and elegance of speech in preaching flies in the face of the cross: "the preaching of Christ crucified is simple and unadorned, and hence it ought not to be obscured by false ornaments of speech."[95] Still, an economy of words does not mean only bare-bones. With Augustine, Calvin points out that "those things which are truly said can at the same time be fittingly said."[96] The point of all this, of course, is accessibility of understanding, and the words and form used must be appropriate both to the scriptural text and to the people hearing them.

    4. Knowing full well (or surely hoping!) that his congregation will generate questions in their minds that in the worship setting have no place for being asked, and for which they cannot also generate the right answers, Calvin asks and answers them for them. As in the commentaries and the *Institutes*, he raises the leading, rhetorical questions: "And why all that?" "But how so?" The effect of this, of course, is to "invite his people into the pulpit" with him, so that they might become more active participants in the event of the proclamation of the Word.[97]

    5. Calvin structures his sentences to require the frequent use of first person pronouns. The first person *plural*, while not missing in the commentary and common in the

Institutes, now dominates. Preaching is a corporate event. God's address to each individual, including the preacher, is in relationship with all present. In this manner he proclaims that all stand under the authority of scripture in the direct line of grace. John Calvin has no special revelation, but preaches under the influence of the same Spirit that works within all believers. By the power of that Spirit alone may God's Word be heard, not only by the preacher, but also by those with whom he or she preaches. Use of the corporate first person underwrites the expectation of active involvement in preaching by all present.

6. Calvin also reveals a distinction in purpose between exegeting in the commentary and *Institutes* and expositing in a sermon. He consistently adds to the exegetical material of the sermon expanded applications *and* gentle exhortations that make it plain how the meaning of the text is to be incorporated into the lives of his hearers. For instance, that "gospel" means "good news" is indeed cause for joy. But it is not license for unrestrained exuberance in the pleasures of this world, ahem. Rather, let us take our delight in Christ. Often Calvin is more specific: "This, in brief, is how we ought to practice this doctrine nowadays."[98]

While the content of both commentary and sermon remains fully didactic, the style varies significantly. The lecturer in the classroom and the author of commentaries becomes in the pulpit both more conversational and more focused on the contemporary realities. In the commentaries Calvin seeks to provide help in understanding the intent and meaning of scripture for use in ministry. In the sermon he transforms this material one step further to make it immediately usable in his peoples' lives. Beyond that, even the casual reader will note in Calvin's sermons a fluidity, and particularly a graciousness, that stand in stark contradiction to his not uncommonly vituperative tracts and treatises. Calvin assumes his people really want to know what it means to be baptized, that while they may be stubborn and hardhearted according to the manner of fallen humanity, they are not so to the degree and intent of the papists and Anabaptists.[99] Nor does he ever assume that just because his people are baptized that they no longer need incessant doses of the healing balm of the gospel. Even the exhortations naturally arise from an attestation to the extraordinariness of God's grace toward us in Christ Jesus. Over and over again one hears in Calvin's sermons the claim of God *pro nobis*, so that no one could leave the pew without having been comforted, filled with good news, *and* empowered to take the next step in the Christian life. Yes, Calvin chastises his people, along with himself, but the predominant note sounds God's persistent, enduring love, here and now, through Christ Jesus. Grounded in that, confirmed in that, then, the baptized can live accordingly, that is, *pro Deo*.

Preaching as a Means of Grace

Thus Calvin's preaching attests to the overall theology we have already seen displayed so clearly. God acts graciously toward us in the face of our limitations and perversities, accommodating the divine self toward our incapacities by speaking to us through media we can understand: human words, human preachers. God's graciousness also takes into account the incapacities of humans as preachers. God provides preachers with the requisite gifts and hearers with the affirmation of ordination that they may be assured that the efficacy of the Word does not, *in fine*, depend on the human preacher. We thus can neither take pride in our preaching or in our preachers. Nor can preachers who preach rightly be blamed for those who fail to hear. The power that lies behind the Word is God, and the power that makes it effective is the Spirit. The only valid question of preachers is whether or not they remain obedient to the call to preach the Word, honoring that ministry by applying to it the fullest use of their God-given abilities.

Again we see how God links the divine self to the human, claiming in the very act of preaching the primacy of God's acts of graciousness toward us in Christ Jesus that alone enables us to respond in faith. God acts in preaching. Therefore, preaching is not *about* grace, but becomes an event, an *act* of grace. Through the Word proclaimed in the corporate setting the individual is brought into dialogical encounter with the substantial Word such that God *pro nobis* is experienced and human life *pro Deo* is enabled. Thus preaching is an occasion of dialogical relationality, the linking of the divine and the human. This is far more evident by virtue of the embodiment of preaching in human persons than it is when one reads privately from Scripture. This again points to the notion, along with the fact that this essential preaching occurs within the church, that being in relationship with God intimately connects with being in relationship with other human beings.

If Calvin can be faulted in his preaching it may well be because he does not accommodate himself *enough* to his hearers. He reveals to us again and again the graciousness of God's acts toward humankind, but it is not at all clear how his hearers can know how to translate that love *as act* from the divine initiative to the human response. Calvin speaks consistently to the intellect and to the will, but greatly neglects, in spite of his awareness that we are corporeal creatures, address of the whole person. In so far as one can know through abstract concepts what it means to live a graced and obedient life, Calvin excels. But he does not give his people enough currency in concrete, particular examples of what that life looks like as it walks the streets of Geneva. Calvin does not lack imagination. He may well lack a more modern pedagogical science that recognizes that we remember far more of what we do than what we see, and more of what we see than hear. But Calvin believes that the faculties of the soul are understanding and will, and understanding is "the leader of the soul."[100] He is convinced that constant appeal to the intellect and the will, with the enlivening of the Spirit, will translate into obedient and correct behavior (among the elect) in the face of even the most confusing ethical decisions. There is no doubt, in any case, that he would attribute any success of his preach-

ing to the work of the Spirit. And, finally, any more explicit
rehearsal of graced reality,[101] in so far as that exists this side
of the eschaton, may be safely left to baptism and the supper.

NOTES

1. 4.1.1.
2. 3.2.4. Calvin notes in the letter to the reader, prefacing the *Institutes*, that his intention in that work is to provide the candidate in theology with help in reading "the divine Word, in order that they may be able both to have easy access to it and to advance in it without stumbling," p. 4.
3. Private reading is insuffcient; rejecting preaching is like "blotting out the face of God..." 4.1.5; also Catechism, p. 130, OS II, p. 129, ¶304
4. 4.1.5
5. 4.1.5
6. 4.1.9, citing Mt. 18:20; 4.8.11.
7. 4.12.5; the church's "blessed and happy state" has its foundation "in the person of Christ," 2.6.2; see also 4.1.2, 3.
8. "...God has chosen the church to be his dwelling place, there is no doubt that he shows by singular proofs fatherly care in ruling it," *Ecclesiam*, OS III, p. 210; 1.17.6.
9. 4.1.4.
10. Calvin's ethical concerns make it equally clear that relationship with God is also normatively expressed *outside* the gathered community in daily Christian life.
11. 4.8.12, citing Paul.
12. 4.1.9, 10; also, "...in it alone is kept safe and uncorrupted that doctrine in which piety stands sound and the use of the sacraments ordained by the Lord is guarded," 4.1. 12.
13. 4.1.21. Forgiveness of sins, for example, "so belongs to the church that we cannot enjoy it unless we abide in communion with the church...it is dispensed to us through the ministers and pastors of the church, either by the preaching of the gospel or by the administration of the sacraments...," 4.1.22. The same thing is true of preaching, baptism, the supper.
14. 4.1.2.
15. 4.1.9, 10, 12, 4.2.1.
16. 4.2. 2-4, 7.
17. 4.1.5.
18. 4.1.10.

19. 4.1.8. Walker wishes to include discipline as one of Calvin's marks, G.S.M. Walker, "Calvin and the Church," in McKim, p. 226, but Calvin himself does not do so. Nevertheless, those whose behavior clearly flies in the face of gospel are excommunicated, 4. 11. 5, see also the "excommunication" in the *Form of Church Prayers, Liturgies of the Western Church*, p. 206; OS II, p. 47.

20. "In this church are mingled many hypocrites who have nothing of Christ but the name and outward appearance," 4.1.7. Calvin distinguishes four types of humans: those who are "(1) endowed with no knowledge of God and immersed in idolatry, or (2) initiated into the sacraments, yet by impurity of life denying God in their actions while they confess him with their lips, they belong to Christ only in name; or (3) they are hypocrites who conceal with empty pretenses their wickedness of heart, or (4) regenerated by God's Spirit, they make true holiness their concern," 3.14.1. Note also the net which gathers all kinds of fish, 4.1.13; and 4.1.14 regarding Corinth.

21. 4.1.2.

22. 4.8.12, 4.1.19; and, "we claim too much for ourselves if we dare withdraw at once from the communion of the church just because the morals of all do not meet our standard or even square with the profession of Christian faith," 4.1.18.

23. 4.1.9

24. 4.9.3-5, 7, 8, 12. Calvin says, unarguably, that all "are somewhat beclouded with ignorance," 4.1.12—perhaps a more gentle critique than humankind deserves.

25. "The pure ministry of the Word and pure mode of celebrating the sacraments are, as we say, sufficient pledge and guarantee that we may safely embrace as church any society in which both these marks exist...some fault may creep into the administration of either doctrine or sacraments, but this ought not to estrange us from communion with the church," 4.1.12, 18, 19.

26. "Some are so necessary to know that they should be certain and unquestioned by all persons as the proper principles of religion. Such are: God is one; Christ is God and the Son of God; our salvation rests in God's mercy; and the like," 4.1.12. Beyond that, and this is essential for Calvin, the determining factor is coherence with scripture, the essence of which is Christ, for of such is the foundation of the Church, 1.7.2, 4.2.1, 5, 4.8.12, 13. See also the editor's note 21, p. 1026-7. Consequently, the church cannot "coin any new doctrine," 4.8.15, 4.9.2, but we are still to listen to the church since "the church makes no pronouncement except from the Lord's Word," 4.8.15. The true church, that is, that recognizes that the church does not authenticate scripture, historical canonization notwithstanding (this is only recognizing the truth for what it is); scripture authenticates the church, 1.7.2. "As if the eternal and inviolable truth of God depended upon the decision of men." 1.7.1.

27. It is this vulnerability to deceit, I believe, that determines the style of Calvin's preaching. He simply is determined to make the truth of gospel readily accessible to any who can hear his sermons. One does not have to be literate to encounter Christ in the Word of God when Calvin is in the pulpit.

28. 4.1.5, 4.3.3, 4.8.2, 4.11.1.

29. 2.6.1, 2.10.4, 3.3.1, 3.3.19, 4.1.5, 4.1.10, 4.1.22, 4.15.4.

30. 4.1.5.

31. All Christ's benefits accompany Christ. 4.14.17, 1.11.7, 2.6.1.

32. Gerrish, "The Word of God...." p. 66.

33. Gerrish, "Gospel and Eucharist," 88 (108). Stauffer claims that true preaching is nothing less than christophany or theophany, Richard Stauffer, "L'Homilétique de Calvin," in *Interprètes de la Bible: Études sur les Réformateurs du XVIe Siècle*. Paris: Éditions Beuchesne, 1980, p. 170.

34. 4.3.3. Determinative is the fact that the power of the Spirit is "present in the continuing preaching of the gospel," 2.15.2.

35. 2.1.4, 3.3.1, 3.4.14, 3.23.13, 3.24.1, 4.1.22, 4.6.4, 4.15.4. Teaching and exhorting describes Calvin's own pattern of preaching that consists of explanation of the text, application to contemporary life, and an exhortation to live accordingly.

36. 4.3.2.

37. 4.1.5.

38. 4.1.5, 4.3.1.

39. 4.3.1, 4.3.3.

40. 4.3.3.

41. 2.5.17, 4.1.1, 5, 6, 4.3.1-3. John H. Gerstner calls this one manifestation of Calvin's two-voice theory of preaching. "John Calvin's Two-Voice Theory of Preaching," in *Articles on Calvin and Calvinism*, Vol. 10: *Ecclesiology, Sacraments and Deacons*. Richard C. Gamble, ed. NY: Garland Publishing, Inc. 1992. But we are assured of this only when the preacher is properly called and ordained.

42. 4.1.5

43. 4.1.10, 19.

44. 4.8.4, also 2.8.46, 3.4.22, 4.8.6. Along with proclaiming the Word goes the office of the keys—all apostles "have been furnished with a common power to bind and loose," 4.6.4, 3.4.21, 4.11.1-2; but they are not to address the responsibilities of magistrates, 4.11.3.

45. 4.8.1ff.

46. 2.2.20, 2.5.5, 3.3.21, 4.1.6, 4.14.10; even the disciples required the assistance of the Spirit, 4.8.8.

47. 4.8.9.

48. 4.11.5.

49. 3.24.13, 3.24.12. Of course it can. Calvin, along with the rest of the Christian tradition, mistakes God's omnipotence to be instrumental power rather than persuasive social power of love—that can indeed be rejected.

50. 3.24.14.

51. 4.1.10, emphasis mine; good seed does fall on impermeable ground, 3.22.10. See also 4.1.6, and above in regard to behavior as evidencing faith and the existence of the true church.

52. Much of Calvin's argument with Rome is based on the failure of its pastors and bishops to preach, 4.2.2, 4.2.10, 4.5.12, 13, 4.7.23. Calvin also notes that "the theologian's task is not to divert the ears with chatter, but to strengthen consciences by teaching things true, sure, and profitable," 1.14.4.

53. Stauffer, 181

54. 4.1.12, 4.9.4.

55. 4.10.26.

56. Cited in Parker, *John Calvin: A Biography*, p. 92; "Le Cinquiesme Sermon sur le Chap. Vl," *Sermons sur le Deuteronome. Seconde Partie* (Sur Les Chap. 11-19; 1555) *loannis Calvini Opera quae supersunt omnia*. Guilielmus Baum, Eduardus Cnitz, and Eduardus Reuss, eds. *Corpus Reformatorum*, Berolini: C.A. Schwetschke et Filium, 1863-1900. Vol. 26, 473ff.

57. 1.9.3

58. The Christian is to open mind and ears "to every utterance of God directed to him" or her; but to cease inquiry where God "sets an end to teaching," 3.21.3. This is certainly applicable to preachers, if not more so. Also, Stauffer notes the Twelfth Sermon on II Tim, (CO, CR LIV, 151) in which scripture is likened to bread to be given in abundance to the hungry—but the crust is too tough for infants—so preachers are to cut it into bite sized pieces! p. 171-2.

59. 1.8.1, 1.11.1.

60. 1.15.4, 2.7.1, 2.8.10, 2.9.3, 2.11.3, 2.16.6, 3.5.9, 4.14.12, 4.17.21, etc.

61. "Epistle to Simon Grynaeus on the Commentary on Romans," in *Calvin: Commentaries*. Joseph Haroutunian, ed. *The Library of Christian Classics, Ichthus* Edition, Philadelphia: The Westminster Press, 1958. p. 76. (CO, CR 38, 403). Scripture presents other problems for us as well. Several authors have pointed out Calvin's recognition of textual errors, e.g.: McNeill, "The Significance of the Word of God for Calvin," p. 144; Gerrish, "The Word of God and the Words of Scripture," p. 63; Rogers and McKim, p. 110-111.

62. 1.13.3.

63. God "prefers to address us in human fashion through interpreters (*interpretes humano*)" 4.1.5, OS V, p. 9; the church is given "the gift of interpretation which sheds light upon the word," 4.17.25. Calvin notes Pauline interpretation of the Old Testament, 2.8.36. One apparent

exception to hermeneutical permission is the *verba Christi*, which "are not subject to the common rule and ought not to be tested by grammar." Yet even this content is still deemed interpretable, 4.17.20.

64. "The Deity of Jesus Christ," in *The Deity of Christ and Other Sermons*, LeRoy Nixon, Tr. Grand Rapids: Wm. B. Eerdmans Publishing Co., 1950, p. 13; CO, CR, 47, 465-484.

65. Calvin commented on all but 9 books of the Old Testament, and Revelation. He depends heavily on Psalms, Isaiah, Matthew, John, Acts, Romans, the Pauline letters, I Peter, and I John. McNeill, p. 136.

66. See, for example, Calvin's address of Mt. 19:21, 4.13.13; the exposition of the decalogue, 2.8.8f; of Christ's prayer, 3.20.36; and the "words of institution," 4.17.20. Note, too, the influence of Calvin's study of law on his exegetical work, Donald K. McKim, "Calvin's View of Scripture," in McKim, p. 48; the influence of Augustine on theology and Chrysostom in exegetical method, Rogers and McKim, p. 114-5 and p. 89f regarding the influence of Humanism. Calvin used all fields of study that were in any way pertinent, including Jewish scholarship, Kraus, p.12; 2.2.16. William J. Bouwsma, *John Calvin: A Sixteenth-Century Portrait*. NY: Oxford U. Press, 1988, reviews the multiple influences on Calvin, along with the tensions he feels they produce.

67. Kraus, p. 13-17. Additional examples of Calvin's exegesis may be seen merely by perusing the *Institutes* or by glancing through the pages of any of the commentaries. Calvin's style varies depending on the type of work he is presenting and his readers and hearers. In the commentaries and in the sermons, for the most part, he works verse by verse; in the *Institutes* this is clearly not the case, except for some particular passages—e.g. Decalogue, Christ's Prayer, *verba Christi*. So his scriptural address ranges from proof-texting (McNeill, p. 136) to full-blown commentary.

68. Epistle to Grynaeus, p. 73.

69. 2.8.1, 8, 11, 17, 3.20.38, 40, 43, 47, etc. A particularly lovely example of clarifying the meaning of a word is Calvin's address of "gospel" in the Introduction to the Commentary on John 1. *The Gospel according to St. John*, p. 5-6.

70. Grynaeus, 73.

71. This concern is most readily seen in the introductions to the commentaries. The phrase is frequently noted within the body of the commentaries, but is not absent from the *Institutes*, e.g., 2.8.18 (God), 3.5.7, 3.20.39.

72. 4.16.23 (*circunstantia*, OS V, p. 328). Kraus translates the last word as "circumstances," which indeed seems more suitable here, p. 16. Examples of his address of setting are his discussion of Nineveh in the Commentary on Jonah 3.3, "The Commentaries of John Calvin on the prophet Jonah," in *Commentaries on the Twelve Minor Prophets*,

Vol. 3. Tr. John Owen. Grand Rapids: Wm. B. Eerdmans Pub. Co., 1950; and as McNeill suggests, in the discussion of Acts 19:2-7, 4.15.18.

73. Kraus, p 14.

74. Perhaps the signal example is Calvin's address of the *Verba Christi* and the troublesome *hoc est corpus meum*, 4.17.20ff; see also his consideration of the names of God, 2.8.18. In the commentary on John, of course, he focuses on *logos*, and its translation by *verbum* (which properly belongs to *hrema*) or *sermo* (p. 5, 8-9).

75. Kraus cites 3.17.14 here, but this is problematic. The Latin text (OS 4, p. 267) as well as the discussion seem better to support item 3. Nevertheless, Kraus' point is valid in that Calvin does exhibit concern for text that precedes and follows a pericope—while at the same time liberally salts any and every argument with fragments of scripture.

76. 2.8.8ff.

77. 2.8.8.

78. 3.20.36ff.

79. See Calvin's identification of the purpose of individual commandments; 3.20.38, 46. So also that the resurrected Christ appears first to women is an attestation that our faith is connected to humility. *Commentary on A Harmony of the Evangelists, Mt. Mk., and Lk.,* Vol 3. Tr. Wm. Pringle. Grand Rapids: Wm. B. Eerdmans Publishing Co, 1949. p. 339.

80. 4.17.20.

81. Preface to Olivétan's New Testament, in *Calvin's Commentaries*, Joseph Haroutunian, ed. *The Library of Christian Classics, Ichthus Edition*, p. 70. The editor notes that this paragraph does not appear in the 1535 edition, but in the 1543 treatise, CO, CR 9, 815. See also 2.11.1ff, 3.20.21. In reference to the Old Testament, Calvin says "it cannot be denied that whenever God declares that He will be propitious to men and forgives their sins, he sets forth Christ at the same time..." *Commentary on St. John.*, p. 5. See also 2.9.2, 3.

82. Calvin cites Paul and Augustine quite regularly, and others of the Christian tradition—either positively or in criticism, 2.8.12, 2.8.28, 3.20.35, 4.17.20ff. Neither does he hesitate to use secular scholars such as Plato, 3.20.34, 4.18.15.

83. Calvin ranges from dry wit, 1.7.1, to outright dripping sarcasm, 1.9.1. See also 1.8.2, 2.7.6, 12. His image of the mirror provides a strong visual component to Calvin's sometimes highly abstract language. Witness also Calvin's effort to clarify how Jonah could possibly go in the opposite direction from that which God wanted. Calvin takes on Jonah's persona, leads his students through an imaginary conversation that Jonah has with himself, then says: "I have no doubt, in my own mind, but that Jonah discussed these things within himself, for he was not a log of wood." "The Commentaries of John Calvin on the prophet Jonah," 1.3, p. 27. Similarly, he speaks of the papists attempt-

ing with their masses to pacify God as one does a baby with a rattle, Sermon IV, Is. 53.7-8, *Sermons on Isaiah's Prophecy of the Death and Passion of Christ.* p. 96
    84. 2.5.19, see also 3.4.5, 4.15.16, etc.
    85. 1.13.3ff.
    86. Letter to the Reader, *Institutes*, p. 4; Introduction to the French edition, *Institutes*, p. 7.
    87. For additional addresses of Calvin and preaching, see Parker, *Oracles*, and T.H.L. Parker, *Calvin's Preaching*, Louisville: Westminster/John Knox for T & T Clark, 1992. Stauffer, Gerstner, and A.G.P. van der Walt, "Calvin on Preaching," *John Calvin's Institutes His Opus Magnum*, Potchefstroom: Potchefstroom University for Christian Higher Education, 1986. Van der Walt makes note of terminology used by Calvin in regard to preaching. Parker includes in *Calvin's Preaching* a number of useful chronologies, catalogues, and other pertinent data.
    88. Other sermons illustrate a looser, freer-flowing movement that tends to conflate, somewhat, the exegesis, explanation, application and exhortation. See, for instance, the sermon on 2 Tim., and the sermons on Isaiah 52.
    89. Augustine, Hilary, Gregory Nazianzus and Erasmus, e.g., are cited in the commentary on v. 1.
    90. Noting puzzlement about the Latin translations of *verbum* for *logos*, which better translates *hrema*; etc.
    91. Regarding *hypostasis*, v.1 in the commentary is related to the Latin *substantia* as Hilary used it, and reference is made to *ta prosopa* and *proprietates*. In the sermon, however, Calvin notes only *hypostasis* without reference to the others.
    92. Parker notes in *Biography* that Geneva is a city full of tradespeople, a middle class community with no millionaires or nobility, p. 54, and certainly few as well-educated and brilliant as Calvin, p. 97.
    93. Calvin's relationship with rhetoric is frequently addressed. See, for example, Parker's *Calvin's Preaching*, Battles' "Accommodating," Rodolphe Peter, "Rhétorique Et Prédication Selon Calvin," *Revue D'Histoire et de Philosophie Religieuses* #2, Vol. 55, 1975. Bouwsma capitalizes on this dimension in Calvin, contrasting it to the classic scholastic approach. He claims that Calvin regularly struggles between these two sides of himself.
    94. Parker, *Calvin's Preaching*, p. 132.
    95. *Commentary on the Epistles of Paul the Apostle to the Corinthians*, p. 76; scripture itself "speaks in the manner of the common folk," 1.11.1; even though we are dealing with "the sublime mysteries of the Kingdom of Heaven," 1.8.1.
    95. 3.23.14. One does question whether some of his invectives against his adversaries were "fittingly said!"
    97. Having composed this statement in 1987-88 for the dissertation form of this work, I was pleased to discover the following in Park-

er's 1992 volume, *Calvin's Preaching*: "In the same way, therefore, as each Christian participates in the activity which is the Lord's (*sic*) supper...so also in the audible sacrament which is the sermon he (*sic*) actively hears and takes into himself (*sic*) the Word of God." p. 48. In the earlier *Oracles*, Parker also notes the expectation that preaching requires the active involvement of the people, p. 61.

98. *Sermons on Isaiah's Prophecy*, 53:1-4, p. 57.

99. Parker notes that even when Calvin was having difficulties with opponents in the congregation, while the sermons may have been more intense in tone, "there is no threshing himself into a fever of impatience or frustration...." p. 116-8. This is certainly not the case in the *Institutes*, where Calvin's temper does flash.

100. 1.15.7.

101. John E. Burkhart, *Worship: A Searching Examination of the Liturgical Experience*, Philadelphia: Westminster Press, 1982, p. 31f.

IV

GOD'S GIFT OF FONT AND TABLE

> *First of all, (God) instituted sacraments, which
> we who have experienced them feel to be highly
> useful aids to foster and strengthen faith. Shut
> up as we are in the prison house of our flesh, we
> have not yet attained angelic rank. God, there-
> fore, in his wonderful providence accommodat-
> ing himself to our capacity, has prescribed a
> way for us, though still far off, to draw near to
> him.[1]*

Still Further Accommodations

We have considered at length God's hunger to be in
relationship with humankind. This is evidenced by the
many ways in which God accommodates the divine self to
our capacity so that we may know that God is for us and
that we are meant to be for God. For Calvin, everything
that constitutes and sustains that multidimensional relationship—the self-knowledge that leads to recognition of God,
the law, the living Christ and the preaching that proclaims
Christ—come to us as gifts of God's graciousness. Gifts,
too, are the Spirit-filled ears and hearts that embrace Christ
and all the benefits Christ brings, and the obedience that
follows. What more could we need? What else could we be
given? And why should we be given anything additional?
Has not God done enough for us?

Calvin would hardly disagree that God has done
enough, far more than enough. But he also recognizes that
we need still more. He has not left us without strong hints

about the "more." However, with our minds bent on knowledge of ourselves and of God, it would be easy to overlook
such hints. Calvin makes a strong appeal to the intellect. He
is himself a brilliant scholar, accustomed to dealing with reality cognitively. It is reason, along with worship, that distinguish us from beasts. For Calvin, the soul's faculties are
understanding and will. Moreover, the proper seat of the
soul is the mind and heart.[2] Calvin accordingly places the
weight of his emphasis on thinking and understanding rather than on feeling or sensing. Believers are to study scripture, because in it we can find everything we need to know
for our salvation. Too, we are to apply to our study all the
legitimate academic disciplines at our command. We are to
learn from teachers in our school, the church, not just until
we reach some magic age, but throughout our entire lives.
Scripture, Christ, the Spirit serve us as pedagogues. This is
heady stuff, conceptual stuff: theory, logic, analysis, cogita-
tion, explanation. Calvin's sermons teach; we must know
God else how can we live in authentic relationship? How
can anyone trust that which one does not know? We must
know.

But minds, intellects, wills do not alone constitute
persons. We live as embodied, enfleshed, whole beings that
relate to our entire world ecosystemically. All the while
Calvin rails at the flesh, despairs of its seductions, its fickleness, nonetheless he knows its integrality to our human
being. God made us enfleshed, after all, even before the
fall. We function physically in a physical world and God
means us to do so. Yes, we are corporeal, frail, limited,
small. And yes, we are called to participate in a spiritual relationship with a transcendent being. Our embodiedness,
because it is fundamental to being human, is nonetheless a
reality with which we must live. Since living means for
Calvin living-with-God, it must therefore mean that God
embraces not just our minds but our whole beings, head to
toe: concepts (knowledge), emotions (prayer, we will see,
is an affection of the heart), the physical senses of eyes,
ears, touch, taste, and smell. Calvin unquestionably grants

ultimate value to the spiritual and that places his recognition of the integrality of human being under significant restraint. His writing reflects this as a matter of some tension for Calvin. But here, too, he walks the middle ground between utter asceticism on the one hand, and utter excess on the other.[3] For all that Calvin himself might prefer angelic form, we are what we are and that is not to be despised. It is as we are in our embodiment that God has claimed us as God's own.

Corporeality

One need only look at the wonder of one's fingers and toes to see the splendor of God. The very cosmos, with its wind, rain, sun and fragrances that we perceive sensually, reveals God's presence. God is to be experienced not merely in thought, and so in the words and deeds of the very humanly enfleshed Jesus of Nazareth we encounter the divine self.[4] Christians, we will learn, are to give alms for those whose bodies will die without food, water, protection from wind and rain and snow and sun. True, gluttony is inappropriate, but so is excessive fasting.[5] The human body needs bread. Water and wine revive it. And one to whom celibacy is *not* given dishonors the body, life, God by attempting to be celibate when marriage is possible.[6]

Not only are we in the first place corporeal, but we are incapable of moving ourselves beyond that very basic state. Precisely because human beings are corporeal creatures with physical needs and fleshly experiences, God expresses incomparable love in a medium we can understand, in plain, simple earthiness, in corporeal forms:

> For if we were incorporeal (as Chrysostom says) (the Lord) would give us these very things naked and incorporeal. Now, because we have souls engrafted in bodies, he imparts spiritual things under visible ones.[7]

How easily we can be swayed by the misery around us unless we also see vividly portrayed and feel with our

fingers things we know can be nothing other than tangible,
utterly real manifestations of divine love for us.[8] But God
intends to live in relationship with us, and in order to bring
us to the divine self, meets us where we are. Once through
the life of Jesus of Nazareth, and now through preachers
and in the events of supper and baptism, in bread and nectar
and water, we have God coming to us on our very earthy
terms, meeting us on our turf, being there for us in our very
physical hunger and thirst and yes, filth. Moreover, God
embraces us as whole beings, as fully integrated both in
ourselves and in terms of our social matrix, once more doing for us what we cannot do for ourselves.[9] The result,
though Calvin might well be uncomfortable saying it so explicitly, is that our spiritual relationship is embodied because we are embodied, even as our embodied relationships
are matters of spirit because we are spiritual beings. We
cannot get away from the weaving that brings polar extremes into absolute intimacy with each other.[10]

God again accommodates the divine self to our need
by blessing us with bread, water, fruit of the vine. These
come to us not as raw elements, base stuff, but sacramentally. Yet these elements are also base stuff, ordinary every-
day things with which we are thoroughly familiar. Calvin
thinks God does not want to overwhelm us here any more
than with the thunder of the divine voice. Yet these ordinary, physical substances at font and table, because they
show forth Christ, possess incredible richness in meaning
and their benefits to us are not readily exhausted.[11] In God's
hands, the mundane becomes the medium of sacrament.

Sacraments as Gifts of God

There is no question for Calvin but that God authors
sacraments.[12] He understands this to be so from scriptural
warrant, for in addressing the "five other ceremonies" proposed by Lombard and held by Rome to be sacraments,
Calvin says, "if we find neither command nor promise,
what else can we do but contradict them?"[13] And, considering the weight Calvin puts on scripture—that it contains all

we need to know for salvation and is therefore the ultimate authority for our lives—this scriptural authority is definitive. But what may be more important, and I think certainly more interesting, is that Calvin recognizes the intrinsic *nature* of sacrament to be gift of God to us. God not only authors sacraments in that God originated them and has commanded us to do them, but most especially, because God is the principal actor in them, God makes promises in them, and in them God acts for our benefit.[14]

Calvin defines the term "sacrament" as embracing "generally all those signs which God has ever enjoined upon men to render them more certain and confident of the truth of his promises."[15] In sacraments God manifests the divine self and "attests his good will and love toward us"[16] in a multitude of ways. Sacraments are thus *testimonies* of God's graciousness on our behalf,[17] they are *signs* and *symbols* of what God does for us,[18] they are *graphic representations* of promises and they make God's mysteries visible.[19] Sacraments are "*mirrors* in which we may contemplate the riches of God's grace,"[20] *seals* or *tokens* that confirm for us all God's good will and work toward us.[21] The content of sacraments is, in fact, the entirety of the promises of God for us.[22] This content is spiritual, yet this spiritual content is communicated through elements that are visible, tactile, olfactory—physical.

Sacraments include much more than elements, more than signs, more than things. Because sacraments have to do with dynamic God *pro nobis*, and therefore with relationship, sacraments are not passive, but active. In them God speaks to us; sacraments announce, tell, ratify God's promises for us and so strengthen our confidence in God *pro nobis*.[23] In fact, sacraments are ceremonies, events,

> exercises which make us more certain of the trustworthiness of God's Word. And because we are of flesh, they are shown us under things of flesh, to instruct us according to our dull capacity, and to lead us by the hand as tutors lead children.[24]

In order to have a sacrament, then, both divine promise as
active presence and human activity must be linked.

Benefits of Sacrament

Through these physical, sacramental events God
"offers us mercy and the pledge of his grace."[25] Because
these things are found and fulfilled for us in Christ, it is
Christ and all Christ's benefits that are offered in sacraments. Christ—not the water, the bread and fruit of the vine
or even the activity—comprises the matter, the substance,
the essence of sacraments.[26] Sacraments show Christ to us,
and lead us directly to Christ.[27] Moreover, Christ presides
in sacraments,[28] and so in them we have immediate access
to all that Christ has to offer: God's incredible graciousness
toward us that includes forgiveness, regeneration, faith,
nourishment.[29] Sacraments, then, are events of relationship
that occur not just in the interchange of human beings
speaking and listening as in the preaching of the Word, but
in the interchange of handing around the basic stuff of life.
Font and table take us another step beyond the cognitive
and sensory experience of hearing to experience through all
our senses. Relationship has to do with whole beings.

No wonder, then that Calvin claims sacraments both
"establish and increase faith,"[30] and indeed stand as "the
pillars of our faith."[31] The Word funds our faith, and sacraments embody gospel in events that include tangible, con-
sumable things, thus providing extra support, stability, and
balance to that faith. At the same time, sacraments participate in the generation of faith. They do so not because they
have some power in themselves, but because God works
through them, because Christ and Christ's benefits are offered through them.[32] Sacraments generate and undergird
our faith because through them God assures us of God's
forgiveness of our sins, by making us confident of God's
enduring love for us in the face of our incapacity, by imparting to us through fundamental, palpable ways the reality and depth and breadth of God's caring for us:

> Indeed, by giving guarantees and tokens
> (Christ) makes it as certain for us as if we had
> seen it with our own eyes. For this very familiar
> comparison penetrates into even the dullest
> minds; just as bread and wine sustain physical
> life, so are souls fed by Christ.[33]

Similarly, the water of baptism signifies that what water
does for the body, the blood of Christ and the Spirit do for
the soul.[34] Sacraments aid faith because they express God's
love for us in terms of our most basic sensory realities of
hunger, thirst and cleanliness. Therein they enable relationship embracing the most primal levels of human being.
How could I not recognize when the water washes over me,
when I swallow bite and sip, that God's nurturing love is
for *me*? What intimate accommodation Calvin's God provides for us!

Relational Presence

We must understand the gift nature of sacraments.
But it is equally critical to recognize the unique relationship
between the giver and that which is present and offered in
sacraments, and the sacramental elements and rites themselves. Sacraments are more than signs, more than things.
They are ceremonies, though not just any kind of ritual ceremony, but events in which Christ is offered and relationship with God is experienced. If Christ is truly offered in
sacraments, if sacraments are events of relationship with
God, God must therefore be truly accessible to us in these
events. But Calvin will have none of the tormenters of poor
Berengarius and their insistence that God's presence is localized in the elements of sacraments.[35] Nor will he accept
the notion of bare or empty signs.[36] Calvin says it is "not
that the gifts set before us in sacraments are bestowed with
the natures of the things, but that they have been marked
with this signification by God."[37] That is, when the words
are added to the elements, something new occurs, but the
elements are not changed in themselves.[38] God is really

present in sacraments, and the effects of that presence are truly available to us, but that presence is totally that of relationship.[39] Neither presence nor effects are by any means reduced to or localized in physical elements, nor ceremonies as a whole.[40] Indeed, Calvin asserts God's constant presence with us, in all of the divine persons. He does, however, reject Luther's doctrine of ubiquity, favoring Augustine's distinction that Christ is omnipresent in majesty, providence and grace, but not in flesh. So also Christ is present everywhere, and particularly in the supper the whole Christ is present, but not in wholeness.[41]

The particular elements of water, bread and grape nectar are the required ones because they are the scriptural ones and because the elements must cohere with the realities they present. If they do not so correspond, there is no sacrament.[42] And, surely because of the signification and because of the relational presence of God, we are to hold in respect the sacramental elements and sacraments as events. But we are not to accord to either the elements or the rites in themselves the honor and reverence that belong to God alone. Divinity is not contained in them any more than it is localized within scripture. Therefore sacramental elements are not to be worshipped any more than the Bible is. Calvin permits idolatry nowhere. Yes, we deal with tangible, concrete, physical, corporeal realities, but we are really dealing with spiritual ones. Yes, God addresses us, relates with us, is present with us around a font full of water and a table laden with the fruit of the earth. But this is so in order that we may move beyond our limited realities to greater ones, that is, to relationship with Godself.

> Indeed, the believer, when he sees sacraments with his own eyes, does not halt at the physical sight of them, but...rises up in devout contemplation to those lofty mysteries which lie hidden in sacraments.[43]

To fail to do this, to let our experience rest only in the moment of the sacrament, or worse, in the physical elements of it, is to commit idolatry, to confuse the gifts for the giver,[44] to mistake the celebration for the relationship. The baptism and joining to Christ does not occur, in fact, in the water, or even in the moment of being baptized. Nor is the fellowship with Christ, the nourishing of faith in the bread and wine, localized in or limited to the moment of celebration. We are not to expect to perceive or experience bread and fruit of the vine or water, or even a whole sacramental event *in se* as the ultimate reality. Rather, we *participate* in the ongoing reality of the goodness of God toward us. This reality is present to the events, but is not bound to, limited to nor wholly enclosed in them. Rather, the presence is spiritual, and the benefits are spiritual, but no less real.[45]

We do not receive imaginary nourishment or even only intellectual nourishment. Although spiritual, we receive real sustenance that can be felt and enjoyed. How is this so? In the same way that it was so in the verbal proclamation of gospel: God makes Godself present and we receive the benefits through the power of God's Spirit, and because the Spirit works *in us*:

> But sacraments properly fulfil their office only when the Spirit, that inward teacher, comes to them, by whose power alone hearts are penetrated and affections moved and our souls opened for sacraments to enter in. If the Spirit be lacking, sacraments can accomplish nothing more in our minds than the splendour of the sun shining upon blind eyes, or a voice sounding in deaf ears.[46]

In the same way that scripture and the preached Word remain useless to us without the Spirit working within us, so also sacraments contain no blessing unless the Spirit empowers us to receive, absorb and benefit from them. By the work of the Spirit, baptism with Word and water, and the supper with Word, bread and nectar become for us authentic, microcosmic but not finished expressions of the ongoing macrocosm of spiritual relationship. So Calvin brings us full circle to sacraments as Augustine defined them: visible signs of sacred things, visible forms of invisible grace.[47]

Beyond this Calvin will not go. There remains an
important dimension of mystery in all this. Although understanding is critical, sacraments are not finally a matter of
science, but of faith. Because they are of God, they always
will be more than we can comprehend. Calvin does not often wax lyrical, but here we can see him finally overcome
by awe issuing forth in almost pure doxology:

> Now if anyone should ask me how this takes
> place, I shall not be ashamed to confess that it is
> a secret too lofty for either my mind to compre-
> hend or my words to declare. And, to speak
> more plainly, I rather experience than under-
> stand it. Therefore, I here embrace without con-
> troversy the truth of God in which I may safely
> rest.[48]

The Certainty of Sacrament

How can we rest here? How can we be assured of
the validity of sacraments, that they are and do what they
say? We know that the truth of scripture as God's Word to
us inheres in itself, and so scripture authenticates itself.
Similarly, the promises sacraments enliven and the relationship they foster authenticate sacraments. That is, the nature
of sacraments as gifts of God's expression of the reality of
God's love for us assures us of the objective validity of sacraments. Moreover, because sacraments are principally
God's gift to us, because God is the primary actor in them,
and because the elements are not identical to the presence
of God, we have no fear of sacraments being either empty
or invalidated for us by a faulty administrator or administration, or by the participation with us of the unworthy.
That is so because

> what God has ordained remains firm and keeps
> its own nature, however men may vary. For
> since it is one thing to offer, another to receive,
> nothing prevents the symbol consecrated by the
> Lord's Word from being actually what it is
> called, and from keeping its own force.[49]

Still, it will not surprise us that the objectively valid nature of sacraments does not guarantee the subjective effect in use. The corrupt or irreverent individual who receives a sacrament needs to attend to Augustine's words: "If you receive carnally, it does not cease to be spiritual but it is not so for you"[50] Sacraments will not work *ex opere operato* in those who reject faith, whose spiritual life with God continues non-existent, who receive sacraments as more or less than they really are.

But are we not all such miserable sinners? "How could we, needy and bare of all good, befouled with sins, half-dead"[51] come either for baptism or supper? What wickedness, what impiety results in condemnation? Dare anyone participate in sacraments? If so, on what grounds? How does one become worthy of the sacramental Word, of the sacraments of font and table, so they can be life-giving for us rather than death-dealing? What of infants, brought to the font without even knowing it? Do they not come already afflicted with sin? Are they then baptized into death, but not life?

In the first place, as was the case with the Word, Calvin understands that the benefits that come from embracing Christ in sacraments are available only to those who have the Spirit at work within. Because the infants of believers already belong to the covenant, they already have a spiritual life because the Spirit works in them from birth at least. Therefore they can and must receive baptism, because what this sign signifies has already occurred.[52] After that, the Spirit leads us to acknowledge our need, enables us to recognize our depravity and frees us to depend on God instead of on ourselves for life. Thus the sole worthiness "which our Lord requires of us is to know ourselves sufficiently to deplore our sins, and to find all our pleasure, joy and satisfaction in Him alone."[53]

God does not ask us to be sinless in order to come to sacraments, claims Calvin. God only asks us to confess our utter incapacity before God and to trust in and surrender to God's gracious love for us. Sacraments will then function for us as "medicine for the sick, solace for sinners, alms to the poor."[54] Baptism will give relief to troubled consciences.[55] The supper will "awaken, arouse, stimulate, and exercise the feeling of faith and love, indeed to correct the defect of both."[56] By the power of the Spirit we receive sacraments in faith that confesses our desperate need and attests God as our only help. Those who sincerely do this are, according to Calvin, welcome at God's font and table and receive there the treasures offered.

This happens only by faith.[57] Depending now on Paul and Titus, Calvin believes that those who despise God, God's claim of life-giving love for us, and God's gift of life-giving relationship, and those who prefer their own designs and rely on their own abilities, whose lives thus are a violation of the love that relationship with God is all about, come only to their death. In the same way that the Word can harden the hearts of the hostile, so the utterly unfaithful who come to sacraments receive what becomes poison for them.[58] Thus we are well advised, says Calvin, to examine our spiritual state, testing our confidence in the salvific accomplishment of Christ, acknowledging commitment to union with Christ and Christ's body, and confessing of the same in word and act.[59]

Fencing the Table

How tragic that, according to Calvin, some might find death at font or table where the extraordinary graciousness of God is the primary claim! But the presence of nonbelievers at such an event holds implications for everyone else who participates. Calvin believes that the admittance of the unworthy to the supper will profane the entire sacrament for us. Now we have already said that the nature of a sacrament makes it always valid *in se*, and so we have no fear of it being invalidated by the wicked or by improper administration. We have further said that our faithfulness through the work of the Spirit makes a sacrament valid *for us*. It is precisely here that the possibility of profanation arises. An obviously impious and wicked life indicates a rejection of God and a dishonoring of Christ. If we admit to sacraments one whose behavior flagrantly exemplifies such rejection, we have in effect assented to their dishonoring of Christ. As a result, we participate in that wickedness, dishonoring Christ ourselves, thereby profaning the sacraments for ourselves by our own faithlessness. Ultimately we may profane the whole church. Because our relationship with the divine as members of the body of Christ, the whole body is at stake here, and with it Christ-self.[60]

This deeply disturbs Calvin. Perhaps it is by way of damage control that he is certain that knowledge is the key, and ignorance is bliss. While Calvin values knowledge everywhere else, here true ignorance of a participant's hypocrisy protects us from harm. We know that the visible church abounds in weeds as well as wheat, but *we are not to conduct examinations of others* to force their sins to the surface. Contrarily, a communicant whose life is known to evidence hostility to God places us in the difficult position of barring him or her from sacraments or suffering the consequences of self-profanation of the gifts and of the whole church. For this reason, and with scripture as support, Calvin justifies the *excommunicatio*, but only for *manifest* adulterers, fornicators, thieves, robbers, seditious persons, perjurers, false witnesses...as well as the insolent."[61]

Now God gives all the divine accommodations precisely so we may be encountered by divine love sufficient to turn our existence into true life or turn our lives around. Yes, the unrepentant have access to the Word. But if the Word and sacraments both show forth and offer Christ, then manifest sinners should be sent away from preaching as well as table, as was true in other times and places. But they are not, for how else may they be encountered by gracious God and led to recognize their need? Furthermore, if sacraments are to provide a clearer, more graspable access to relationship (Calvin's very argument for God's use of basic physical stuff) are the impious not, by being limited to the preached Word, asked to benefit from a doctoral program before they have graduated from kindergarten? How will they ever be overwhelmed by grace? How will they ever experience what has been so important for Calvin, the astoundingly loving God who repeatedly bends over backward to meet us *where we are* amid our fragility and failure? Even if these are the ones predestined to hell, is not God the only arbiter of that? Yet Calvin was steeped in classic theology before encountering humanism, and it is not surprising that he cannot quite see how accommodatingly gracious God really is. In Strasbourg, apparently all were invited to the table, and Bullinger deemed even a warning by way of fencing the table was inconsistent with the celebrative character of communion. But Geneva was not Strasbourg, and context matters, particularly in a city whose Christian life was deemed especially inadequate.[62] Perhaps more important is Gerrish's claim that Calvin was attempting to protect both sacrament and church from "a mentality that reduces the sacred signs to mere reminders, communion with Christ to beliefs about Christ, and the living body of the church to an association of like-minded individuals."[63] In the end, Calvin comes off no worse with this dilemma than most of Christendom. He is better about it than many when he comes to the manner in which bath and meal should be celebrated.

The Manner of Celebration

Because we are vulnerable, limited, easily confused and misled, and because sacraments truly offer Christ and attest to others our relationship with God, we need to celebrate sacraments with decorum.[64] Calvin understands that in order to insure propriety God has made the administration of events at font and table, like the preaching of gospel, a function of ecclesial ministry. Pastors and teachers own the responsibility of seeing to our correct understanding of sacraments so that we know what we are doing, or rather, what God is doing. It is the task of pastors to guarantee the decency, dignity, order of sacraments, lest we participate in sacraments casually, inappropriately, dishonorably, destructively, and thereby destroy the peace and unity of the church.[65] As with all ceremonies, simplicity is key, since "great heaps of ceremonies" tend to overwhelm the weak, and that helps no one. Simplicity serves clarity, and undoubtedly that is why the apostles modelled it.[66]

As we know, Calvin opposes the imposition of particular forms or texts, but he does propose patterns for the celebration of sacraments:

> How much better it would be to omit from baptism all theatrical pomp, which dazzles the eyes of the simple and deadens their minds; whenever anyone is to be baptized, to present him to the assembly of believers and, with the whole church looking on as witness and praying over him, offer him to God; to recite the confession of faith with which the catechumen should be instructed; to recount the promises to be had in baptism; to baptize the catechumen in the name of the Father and of the Son and of the Holy Spirit; lastly, to dismiss him with prayers and thanksgiving. If this were done, nothing essential would be omitted; and that one ceremony, which came from God, its author, not buried in outlandish pollutions, would shine in its full brightness.[67]

Calvin goes on to explain that he is not concerned about the particular method of applying water. He does believe immersion to have been the practice in antiquity, but seems disinterested in claiming it as a norm for the Geneva churches. Perhaps this results from his concern for simplicity, since immersion in churches with small baptismal fonts promises to be quite complicated indeed. More likely, however, this falls under the category of not burdening consciences with requirements that scripture does not make.[68] Calvin knows perfectly well how often "norms" get transformed into mandates. He does, however, offer suggestions for the celebration of the supper:

> First, then, it should begin with public prayers. After this a sermon should be given. Then, when bread and wine have been placed on the

Table, the minister should repeat the words of
institution of the Supper. Next, he should recite
the promises which were left to us in it; at the
same time, he should excommunicate all who
are debarred from it by the Lord's prohibition.
Afterward, he should pray that the Lord, with
the kindness wherewith he has bestowed this sacred food upon us, also teach and form us to receive it with faith and thankfulness of heart,
and, inasmuch as we are not so of ourselves, by
his mercy make us worthy of such a feast. But
here either psalms should be sung, or something
be read, and in becoming order the believers
should partake of the most holy banquet, the
ministers breaking the bread and giving the cup.
When the Supper is finished, there should be an
exhortation to sincere faith and confession of
faith, to love and behavior worthy of Christians.
At the last, thanks should be given, and praises
sung to God. When these things are ended, the
church should be dismissed in peace.[69]

If this seems spare to some, Calvin permits additions that
enhance the dignity of the meal, assuming such amend-
ments do not obscure its meaning.[70] We may suspect his
own caution regarding the burdening of consciences functions as a bridle, as he might say, against his inclination to
insist on the less-is-more approach.

Sacraments are intended to unite us to Christ and
thus to each other. Baptism signals our engrafting into the
body of Christ, while the supper signifies our unity by
bread of many grains mixed together, and by our obvious
corporate participation. Sacraments are essential to creating
fellowship out of quantitative connectedness, and are to attest that fellowship. Consequently, private celebrations are
not fitting, since they repudiate and destroy the unity of the
church.[71] But corporate celebrations also must occur in such
a way that does not destroy or belie the unity of anyone to
Christ or members of the body to each other. Beyond that,
sacraments are to be shaped by the same criteria as is all
worship, but with the particular requirement that the signs
used be consistent with the reality signified. The bottom

line remains that our sacramental practice, however we design and implement it, must reveal Christ clearly and manifest Christ's benefits. Our experience with bath and meal is
meant to be experience of God's incredible love for us and
of our being gathered into loving relationship with God and
one another. Calvin never lets go of the notion that God's
loving, accommodating way with us serves as the paradigm
for our living with others.

The Human Role in Sacraments

In Calvin's view, God provides sacraments for our
benefit. Only in so far as they accomplish God's goal of
enabling us to live in relationship with the divine, do they
benefit God. Of the supper Calvin notes, "the very powerful and almost entire force of the Sacrament lies in these
words: 'which is given *for you*,' and 'which is shed *for
you*'."[72] So also baptism, which attests God's love for us
and thereby offers us blessed assurance of divine benevolence. Sacraments present God at work *pro nobis*, here,
now, in personal as well as corporate address. God does not
need sacraments, but we do, for the building of faith and
for the building of the body. Intrinsically, sacraments can
never be our response to the preaching of the Gospel, nor
work that we do. Rather, with the Word preached, the
events at table and font embody God's address, God's gift,
God's coming to us. We do not offer God gifts in sacraments, and the meal is certainly *not* a sacrifice to God.
Quite the contrary. God offers us gifts of life in them. So
Calvin pointedly remarks: "There is as much difference between (the sacrifice of the Mass) and the sacrament of the
Supper as there is between giving and receiving."[73] Yes, we
bring our children for baptism, but baptism fundamentally
enacts God's gracious faithfulness, not ours. Yes, we
should receive the supper with thanksgiving, says Calvin,
and indeed, we cannot receive it without the sacrifice of
praise. Therefore, the meal is not fundamentally *our* Eucharist, *our* thankful gift to God, but *God's* Eucharist,
God's *good gifts*[74] that enliven us and empower us to live a

life of *eucharistia*, a life of thanks and obedience when the
supper is over and we are at work in the world.[75]
Calvin has not forgotten that faith is relationship,
that we live in dialogue with God. And he recognizes that
dialogue in the events of font and table just as he did in the
preaching of the Word. While God is the primordial actor
in sacraments, we are the ones who body them forth. Nor
does Calvin ignore the fact that everything we do and endorse in the church makes a theological statement to ourselves and to the world:

> the signs here given are ceremonies ... testimo-
> nies of grace and salvation from the Lord so
> from us *in turn* they are marks of profession, by
> which we openly swear allegiance to God, bind-
> ing ourselves in fealty to him.... Hence you can
> rightfully say that such sacraments are ceremo-
> nies by which God wills to exercise his people,
> *first*, to foster, arouse, and confirm faith within;
> *then*, to attest religion before men.[76]

Christians do not participate in sacraments primarily
to effect such a confession; rather, confession simply results from our participation. It is the first of two outward results. The second is that of responsibility toward others. Because sacraments are sacraments of unity, not only must we
celebrate sacraments in ways which reflect that, we must
also live eucharistically. Neither the sacrifice of thanksgiving nor that of praise has anything to do with appeasing
God, acquiring forgiveness, or meriting righteousness, but
with the proper worship of glorifying God as a result of
God's love toward us. In point of fact, Calvin outlines three
uses of the supper: (1) everything that God does to feed our
faith, (2) confession, and (3) "a kind of exhortation for us"
to all the duties of love.[77] *Our* eucharist, suggests Calvin,
consists in living out the claim of the sacraments that in
them we are bound together, such that

> none of the brethren can be injured, despised,
> rejected, abused, or in any way offended by us,
> without at the same time, injuring, despising,

> and abusing Christ by the wrongs we do....we
> ought to take the same care of our brethren's
> bodies as we take of our own; for they are mem-
> bers of our body....[78]

In other words, our every-day life needs to evidence God's love for us, and our love for God in care for our neighbor.

Neither the confession nor the life of loving others could result if they were not given us by God, since all that we have that is good, right and faithful, originates in God. So Calvin ultimately maintains the emphasis on what God does in sacraments. He does so not simply as a counter-argument to Rome, but because to emphasize what *we* do in sacraments would be sacrilege and idolatry. As well, Calvin has no desire to release us from our responsibility to live eucharistically in the world by doing for our neighbor what God has done for us. If we faithfully participate in the supper, we must also faithfully participate in living out our thanks in caring for those in need.

Word, Font, Table

It should be evident by now that the content and functions of meal and bath are precisely the content and functions of preaching. In fact, Calvin says quite plainly, "let it be regarded as a settled principle that sacraments have the same office as the Word of God: to offer and set forth Christ to us, and in him the treasures of heavenly grace."[79] Because the Word contains the promises of God and offers Christ; because the content of the events at table and font consists of the promises of God and the Christ in which they are found and fulfilled, sacraments are inextricably bound to the Word. There can be no sacrament without the Word of promise preceding it, without the offer of Christ that the Word offers. Sacraments are what they are because they are filled with the Word.[80] They teach nothing other, seal nothing other, mirror nothing other, embody nothing other than the promises of the Word. Indeed, sacraments are made up of two parts: the promise of the Word, and the physical form.[81] But, as Calvin says,

> let us understand that these words are living
> preaching which edifies its hearers, penetrates
> into their very minds, impresses itself upon their
> hearts and settles there, and reveals its effective-
> ness in the fulfilment of what it promises.[82]

Calvin does not mean just the "words of institution," the
command, spoken as warrant, but the preached word when
he says sacraments cannot exist without the Word.[83] Sacraments require preaching so we will rightly understand as
much as we possibly can. Similar to the way, then, that the
gifts of baptism and supper are accommodations added to
the preaching of the Word, we can also see, conversely,
how preaching functions as an accommodation to our inability to comprehend the events in which we participate.
We are whole persons. Experiencing and receiving sensually the promised gifts of God in table-sharing and baptism
cannot suffice. Indeed, as the medieval mass shows, it fos-
ters superstition. But with preaching the symbols and our
senses and imagination do not have to carry all the weight,
because preaching will elucidate for our cognitive dimension what is happening to us. Our souls, in Calvin's view,
cannot depend on osmosis via senses; we must be encountered intellectually. This is necessary precisely because
these events point to another reality than their own visible
one, and therefore a "sacrament requires preaching to beget
faith."[84] It is the meaning, the deep content of baptism, the
relationship that "draws us away, not only from the visible
element which meets our eyes, but from all other means,
that it may fasten our minds upon Christ alone."[85] If we do
not recognize that meaning in the sacrament, we will be
lost in idolatry and cut off from the fellowship of God.[86]
Preaching takes on the task of lifting up the meaning of the
sign, the ceremony, so that we know what the drama in
which we engage portrays for us. We have to know, says
the scholar, how Christ is made ours in order to possess
Christ and enjoy the benefits Christ brings. If we do not understand, we cannot know what this business of relation-

ship is about and cannot live it.[87] Still, preceding supper or
baptism with preaching is only the usual pattern,

> the ordinary arrangement and dispensation of
> the Lord which he commonly uses in calling his
> people—not, indeed, prescribing for him an un-
> varying rule so that he may use no other way.
> He has certainly used such another way in call-
> ing many, giving them true knowledge of him-
> self by inward means, that is, by the illumina-
> tion of the Spirit apart from the medium of
> preaching.[88]

Infant baptism provides one obvious example. Calvin's basic claim is that the children of Christian parents
are heirs by birth to the promises given to the community
of the faithful, and thus should not be excluded from the
sign. While preaching precedes baptism with the regard to
the parents, it follows it in regard to the infant. This is not
so in the case of the supper, because of the possibility of
self-condemnation through lack of discernment of the body.
Of course, if both sacraments in fact have the capacity to
generate faith through the action of God in them, (which is
to say that discernment of the body occurs in the act of participation), there is no excuse whatsoever for excluding infants from the meal. But it also remains that preaching and
table-sharing and preaching and baptism belong together
because of their intrinsic relationship and for the sake of the
whole body

Similarities and Distinctions.

Yet the events of embodying gospel in preaching
and at table or font are not identical. They are integrally related because their objective essence is the same: both offer
Christ. But their manner of offering is different, and in that
sense, each serves the other on our behalf. We see a dialogical relationship here, for all the while meal and bath confirm the Word of promise for us, the promises are busy
confirming bath and meal. The latter depend on the word of

command and promise, the preached word.

    Is the Word, then, dependent on sacraments? Not at all, but we are. A sacrament

> is not so much needed to confirm (God's) Sacred Word as to establish us in faith in it. For God's truth is of itself firm and sure enough, and it cannot receive better confirmation from any other source than from itself.[89]

The "more" of sacraments in relation to the preaching of gospel does not rest fundamentally in *their* nature as gift, in their content of Christ, in their function of offering Christ. The "more" of sacraments has rather to do with *our* nature as limited and yes, corporeal, human beings. The activities at table and font do not do anything other than the preached Word does, but because of our need, they do it differently: more clearly, tangibly, holistically.[90] They do this precisely because God honors and therefore accommodates the divine self to our corporeal reality, because God has made us whole beings replete with more senses than merely the auditory, and because our physicality enables us to recognize the spiritual more readily if it is incorporated in tangibles. Ironically, Calvin misses the fact that preaching is also a physical, tangible act in which the whole community participates! Therefore, although Calvin did not do so, we can call right preaching, the offering of relationship with Christ through the corporeal means of the human preacher, sacrament.[91]

    Calvin does admit that one's justification does *not* depend on one's participation in sacraments:

> For we know that justification is lodged in Christ alone, and that it is communicated to us no less by the preaching of the gospel than by seal of the sacrament, and without the latter can stand unimpaired.[92]

Sacraments remain normative for us because we need every help available to us in order that we might live in healthy

relationship with God. For Calvin the life of faith is barely
possible for us in the first place, and to help us with that
God has graciously granted us these aides. Calvin is equally
convinced that to cut oneself off from such helps is nothing
else than sheer folly, for "since in (the sacred feast) Christ
is given to us as food, we understand that without him we
would pine away, starve, and faint—as famine destroys the
vigor of the body."[93] Who would not wish to have regular
access to the fountain of life? In the catechism, Calvin is
stronger:

> M: If it is true that God instituted sacraments
> to be an aid to our necessity, should it not be
> rightly condemned as arrogance, that anyone
> should judge himself able to do without them as
> though they were unnecessary?
> C: Certainly. Hence if anyone abstain volun-
> tarily from their use, as if he had no need of
> them, he holds Christ in contempt, rejects his
> grace, and quenches the Spirit.[94]

At the same time, the nature of covenant and the fact that
the absence of the sign does not invalidate the promise
maintains the safety of those who for a legitimate reason
cannot be properly baptized before death.[95]
    So Calvin encourages us to remind ourselves that
we are baptized, and that we cannot deprive infants of the
faithful of the same sign without effectively cutting them
off from the family.[96] Likewise Calvin commends us to frequent and regular use of the supper, both because of what is
provided for us there, and because in so doing we re commit our lives to life in relationship with God.[97] In other
words,

> the Lord's Table should have been spread at
> least once a week for the assembly of Chris-
> tians, and the promises declared in it should
> feed us spiritually. None is indeed to be forcibly
> compelled, but all are to be urged and aroused;
> also the inertia of indolent people is to be re-
> buked. All, like hungry men should flock to
> such a bounteous repast.[98]

And yet this does not apply to baptized infants, however, since Calvin perceives them to be too young to discern the body and thus to participate in this particular feast. Infants, Calvin thinks, are fed otherwise, according to their capacity.[99]

If preaching and sacraments are not identical to each other, neither is baptism identical to the meal. They are both, of a certainty, gifts of God in origin. They have the same essential content of Christ, with God as the primary actor, Christ as the presider, and the gathered community as the context. They result in the same things: generating and nourishing faith. The supper is a "remembrancer (*sic*), or memorial" of Christ's death and a seal of the assurance of pardon. But baptism is a memorial also.[100] Each sacrament manifests unity: baptism as a sign of our incorporation in faith in Christ, the supper as an attestation of unity "in true doctrine and love."[101] They are, in effect, confessional both verbally and in a eucharistic life.

Each sacrament also possesses characteristics that are, if not unique to it, more particular to it than to the other. The symbols, of a certainty, are exclusive to each, and directly related to the sacrament's major claim. Baptism's forte is its attestation of God's initial embrace of us, of the cleansing that effects our incorporation into the body of Christ. In this it replaces circumcision, and as such it is not repeatable.[102] Similarly, baptism is the essential Christian vow, though the vow is implicit in infants and must be embraced when one is capable of comprehending it. It can be said that each time one participates in the supper, this vow is claimed anew.[103]

Calvin places much emphasis on baptism as signifying our ongoing mortification and regeneration.[104] Yet it seems that the meal, perhaps more subtly, makes the same claim, if we come to it in humility and in need. The Supper most vividly portrays God's ongoing, life-giving sustenance and nurture of us, and so we are invited to the table again and again and with a regularity akin to the meeting of our physical needs for sustenance and nurture.[105] The possibility of profanation and poisoning belong especially to the supper, and here Calvin most explicitly names the distinction between the two sacraments, specifically, between the meal and infant baptism. That is, the supper is given to those who have the capacity for solid food. For infants, as noted above, Calvin believes baptism suffices until they are able to discern the body. In his view they are fed otherwise by Christ, and exclusion from the table does not exclude them from the community, although in practice as well as in theory this is simply not true.

A Multi-Dimensional Weaving

If there were any doubt prior to our address of sacraments, Calvin clearly attests that God relates with us as whole beings, and seeks a relationship that is not limited to what to us is purely conceptual, but embraces fully the experiential. Faithful Christians do not only think about or know about God in our heads, we experience God's love for us and body it forth in our daily living. The "recognition of him consists more in living experience than in vain and high-flown speculation, says Calvin."[106] Thus he demonstrates that he understands that God reveals the divine self in nature to our senses of touch, smell, sight and ear; in words that are seen and heard in a whole life (Jesus') that is lived out in the matrix of human interaction and relationship. But we are limited, corporeal, and experience iife in the present moment. So a once-upon-a-time even as a once-for-all-time bodying forth of God's love for us leaves us struggling for visible, tactile, experiential expressions of the reality *hic et nunc*. Therefore God blesses us with sacraments that mirror that spiritual reality and, by assuring us of it, enable us to participate in it.

Again and again we learn not only of God's initial accommodation to our desperate need, but the ongoing reality, the ongoing dialogue. Even though our flesh, our corporeality, is considered to be saturated with our depravity, even though that flesh is ultimately to be transformed to spirituality, God nonetheless meets us there, comes to us where we are, and offers us life here, now, as well as then.

The same dialogical construct is reflected in sacraments that are grounded in promises and are confirmed by promises, yet themselves confirm those same promises. We see, too, the curious conversation between signs that are not what they signify but nonetheless enable our experience of what they signify, between sacraments that are not things, but events of relationship. Likewise we discover the unresolved tension between ceremonies that we embody, that become our confession—but do so because they are first and foremost God's gifts to us. As with the preached Word, we have the linkage of faith and sacrament. Like the Word, events at font and table are always valid objectively because of their nature as gifts of God. But they are valid for us only when received in faith. More, sacraments require faith and yet generate faith, and the Spirit is the one who makes the paradoxical process work. No, sacraments are not required for justification, but our faith is so shaky that without them we really cannot be bound to Christ and nourished in fellowship with God and with others. Yet children must do without the help of the meal.

No wonder Calvin finally throws up his hands in surrender to mystery. All the discrete categories, all the neat boundaries, all the two-dimensional, either-or thought patterns have dissolved in an intricate, multi-dimensional weaving in which threads can be traced but not separated out. This can only, finally, be God's doing, God's active, ongoing interaction with limited, fickle, vulnerable, worthless but nonetheless deeply loved and therefore of infinite worth human beings.

Personal Address, Inter-Personal Commitment

But there remains another interesting dimension to sacraments that is implied but barely stated in Calvin's discussion of them. Calvin quite clearly recognizes that God addresses humanity in general. God's self-attestation in the cosmos and in preaching speaks collectively to whomever may be present (albeit presumably hardening the hearts of some) via the Old Testament Covenant community and in the Church as the body of Christ. But we note also an extremely and intensely personal dialogue between us and God, first through the Spirit, who works in each of us individually, but most especially through sacraments. After all, it is quite conceivable that the anguished soul might fail to understand that God *pro nobis* includes her or himself in particular. So God accommodates yet again, addressing us finally not as "resident," or "to whom it may concern." It is my name that is called, my whole self that is embraced, and this never more so than in sacraments, where bread and wine are placed in my own hand, and my own mouth; where water is poured over my head and my name is bound immediately to God's name. In the experience of nature, in the reading of scripture, in the hearing of the Word preached, doubt may have prevailed about whether or not divinity in fact had the unique, solitary me in view. In the sacramental event God *pro nobis* becomes undeniably *pro me* here and now.

Yet this is not the end, but the beginning. Calvin insists that as certainly as God addresses and claims and nurtures each one of us, the effect of that is not merely a fundamental relationship with God. We are covered with the grime of sin and guilt, yes, and God washes us and makes us clean and new again. We are hungry, yes, so God feeds us. We are thirsty, yes, so God restores and refreshes us with enlivening nectar. Again, and again, and again. But we know that life with God means loving relationship with others. Sacraments as inter-relational, unity-generating events model that. In baptism we are joined to Christ and thus united to the whole fellowship of the baptized. What we receive from the hands of God in the supper we are to receive with thanksgiving, with a eucharistic life, with giving of bread and wine and forgiveness over and over and over again to those in the pew next to us and in the world in which we live.

We have earlier proposed that God's incessant attention to us in our miserable state attests not, finally, to our worthlessness, but to our worth in God's eyes. Yes, Calvin rails against the limitations and lusts of the flesh. Yet he understands that in the gifts of the sacrament, that claim of God's love for us becomes immediate and concrete. It becomes corporeal because we are corporeal, and because we are whole persons who relate to the world and to our neighbors with all our senses. This transcendent God becomes accessible to us by way of earthy means, in terms of basic human needs: cleanliness, hunger, thirst; in plain, ordinary water, staff of life bread and exotic, enlivening, wine. God does this not with reservation, but with the generosity and wisdom of a loving parent. Surely "we must prove our ungratefulness to him if we did not in turn show ourselves sons....we must take care that God's glory shine through us...."[107]

NOTES

1. 4.1.1.
2. 1.3.3, 1.15.7, 2.2.2, 2.2.17.
3. See McKim, "John Calvin: A Theologian for an Age of Limits," 295ff, and Bouwsma, especially p. 89 and 134ff.
4. 1.10.2, 4.17.32. See Balke, "The Word of God and Experientia According to Calvin," for his exposition of this concept.
5. 3.19.9, 4.12.15, 18.
6. 4.12.22ff, 4.13.17, 18, 21.
7. 4.14.3, 6, 4.17.1
8. 4.17.8.
9. That Calvin understands the civic order to be theologically based attests to this concept even further, 4.20.1ff.
10. Bouwsma repeatedly notes how much Calvin despises "mixtures" and seeks purity in every dimension. He also shows how Calvin emphasizes "decorum"—moderation—and remains in himself and in many theological arenas thoroughly, if not well, mixed.
11. 4.10.14, 4.14.4.
12. 4.14.1ff, 4.15.1ff, 4.16.1, 4.17.1, 4.18.19, 4.19.2, etc. By God's authority alone sacraments are celebrated in the church.
13. 4.19.1ff, 4.14.3. The ceremonies are Confirmation, Penance, Marriage, Ordination, Extreme Unction.

14. God provides for God's family, 4.1.1,10, 4.14.1, 5ff, 4.17.1, 4.18.19.

15. 4.14.18. See also 4.14.13 on the term *sacramentum*.

16. 4.14.6, 22, 4.17.1, 4.18.19.

17. 4.14.1, 7, 22, 4.19.2; baptism is a testimony of our union with Christ and sharing in Christ's blessings, 4.15.6; the supper that Christ's life is poured into us, 4.17.10.

18. 4.14.1; Baptism "is the symbol of forgiveness of sins," 3.4.6; and the sign of initiation into the church, 4.1.20, 4.15.1. John Riggs notes the 4.1.20 claim about initiation appears in the 1539 edition of the *Institutes*, but not until 1543, when Calvin seeks to clarify his ecclesiology, does it turn up in the section on Baptism itself. John W. Riggs, "Emerging Ecclesiology in Calvin's Baptismal Thought, 1536-1543," *Church History* Vol. 64, #1, March 1995. Baptism "points to" our cleansing from sin, the mortification of our flesh, 4.16.2. Bread and wine are signs and symbols of Christ's body and blood, 4.17.1, 3, etc. Note that matter and sign are linked but distinguishable, and must be distinguishable. No transubstantiation occurs, nor are sacraments empty signs, 4.14.15,17, 4.15.2, 4.17.10-12,14, and below. However, the name of the thing is given to the sign (metonymy) 4.17.10, 21, 23.

19. 4.14.1, 5, 12, 4.17.10, 14. The signs must correspond to the reality they image, 4.17.14.

20. 4.14.3, 6.

21. 4.14.1, 5-7, 12, 14, 20, 4.15.1, 4.16.9, 4.17.5, 10, 4.19.2.

22. 4.14.1, 4, 6, 12, 16, 18, 20, 4.15.5, 4.17.4, 4.18.19. There is no sacrament without a preceding promise, 4.14.3, 4, 4.18.19—hence the "other five ceremonies" can not be sacraments, 4.19.1 ff.

23. 4.14.10, 17.

24. 4.14.6, 19, 4.19.33. That sacraments are exercises leading us to God is beautifully illustrated by the *Form of Church Prayers,* that from start to finish answers the recognition of human depravity and need with claims of the graciousness of God toward us, leading finally to the climax of the supper as a whole-person, whole-community experience of the intimate, dialogical relationship with God. The final prayer functions as a hinge to move this experience out into the world.

25. 4.14.7, 3.3.11, 19.

26. In fact, "Christ is the matter or (if you prefer) the substance of all the sacraments: for in him they have all their firmness, and they do not promise anything apart from him." 4.14.16, 4.15.2, 6, 4.17.5; "When I wish to show the nature of this truth in familiar terms, I usually set down three things: the signification, the matter that depends upon it, and the power or effect that follows from both. The signification is contained in the promises, which are, so to speak, implicit in the sign. I call Christ with his death and resurrection the matter, or substance. But by effect I understand redemption, righteousness, sanctification, and eternal life, and all the other benefits Christ gives to us." 4. 17. 11, 33;

the gifts offered in baptism are the gifts of Christ, 4.15.6. "Christ is the only food of our soul," 4.17.1.

27. 4.10.14, 4.14.20ff, 4.15.2, 4.17.11, 18, 4.18.11, 3.11.9. All ceremonies, not just sacraments, are to accomplish the same goal of showing forth and leading to Christ.

28. 4.14.9, 4.14.17, 4.15.8, 14, 16, 4.17.1, 10, 18, 32. Therefore, it should make no difference who administers a sacrament. However, Calvin restricts the celebration of sacraments to duly ordained males not, he claims, because of the sacraments' intrinsic nature, but because of his understanding of what is required for the maintaining of order, 4.15.20-22. Calvin does not question patriarchy in this regard.

29. 4.14.7, 9, 10, 12, 19, 4.15.1, 5, 11, 12, 14, 17, 4.17.1, 5, 10, etc. We recall also Calvin's conviction of a partially realized eschatology, so that while sacraments attest these realities as now ours, we still continue to struggle against sin, 3.3.9, 10, 14, 4.1.22, 4.15.11, 4.17.42.

30. 4.14.9, *stabiliendam*, OS V, 266; "sustain, nourish, confirm, and increase," 4.14.7, 10, 12, 18; foster, confirm, increase knowledge of Christ, 4.14.16; baptism arouses, nourishes, confirms faith, 4.15.14, while infants are baptized into future repentance and faith, 4.16.20; the supper nourishes, strengthens, refreshes, gladdens, 4.17.1, 3; and is "to awaken, arouse, stimulate, and exercise" faith and love. In fact, this "feast is medicine for the sick, solace for sinners, alms to the poor...." 4.17.42.

31. "...faith rests upon the Word of God as a foundation; but when sacraments are added, it rests more firmly upon them as upon columns," 4.14.6.

32. 4.14.17. Gerrish rightly insists upon the concept of instrumentality as essential to Calvin's theology of sacrament, *Grace and Gratitude*, p. 167. See below on the necessity of the Spirit to the effectiveness of sacraments.

33. 4.17.1, 10, 18.

34. 4.15.2, 4.16.25.

35. 4.17.10ff, and editor's note #32; 4.17.19ff. Berengar of Tours, an eleventh century scholastic theologian opposed to the doctrine of transubstantiation, was compelled to confess that "the bread and wine after consecration are the real body and blood of our Lord Jesus Christ, not merely the sacrament thereof; and that body is sensibly, not merely sacramentally, but in reality (*sensualiter, non solum sacramento, sed in veritate*), handled by the priest's hands and crushed by the teeth of the faithful." Geoffrey Wainwright, *Doxology: The Praise of God in Worship, Doctrine and Life; A Systematic Theology*, NY: Oxford University Press, 1980, p. 260.

36. 4.14.15, 17, 4.17.10, 11. Calvin points out Augustine's two vices in regard to sacraments: (1) receiving the signs as empty; (2) confusing the signs with the reality, 4.14.16. Both vices evidence lack of faith.

37. 4.14.3, 4.15.14, 4.17.20, 21.
38. 4.17.14, 15.
39. 4.14.17, 4.17.13.
40. 4.15.2, 4.17.19, 4.14.17, 4.16.2, 4.17.39.
41. 4.8.11, 4.17.30, 4.17.23ff, 26. This is so by the power of the Spirit.
42. 4.15.2, 4.17.11, 14, 15, 18.
43. 4.14.5, 4.15.2, 4.17.11, 18, 20ff, 29, 35-37.
44. 4.17.36.
45. 4.14.10, 12, 4.15.3, 5, 14, 4.17.1ff.
46. 4.14.9, 4.14.8, 10, 17, 4.15.6, 4.17.10ff.
47. 4.14.1.
48. 4.17.32. Gerrish finds Calvin's parsing of the relationship between sign and thing signified ultimately unsatisfactory, *Grace and Gratitude*, p. 13.
49. 4.14.16, 4.14.7, 4.15.3, 16, 4.17 33; this appears to be contradicted in 3.14.7, and in Calvin conversation about excommunication. We consider this further below.
50. 4.14.16.
51. 4.17.42.
52. 4.15.20, 4.16.5-7, 15, 17-21.
53. *Form of Church Prayers*. Thompson, 207; OS II, 47-48; we are to bring our unworthiness, our depravity, our humility, 4.17.42. Acts of contrition and expiation cannot make us worthy, only God can, 4.17.41. See also 4.16.30(1).
54. 4.17.42, 4.15.3.
55. 4.15.4, 10, 11, 4.16.32.
56. 4 17.42.
57. 3.24.17, 4.14.7, 15-17, 4.15.15, 17, 4.17.5; "1 deny that (the supper) can be eaten without some taste of faith," 4.17.33. But note also that sacraments can generate faith, above.
58. Calvin depends on the Pauline text of I Cor. 11:29; see 4.1.15, 4.4.6, 4.16.30, 4.17.34, 40, 41. He compares this with the experience of feeding an upset stomach. The toxins in the stomach spoil what is otherwise perfectly good food, and cause the person further harm (Titus 1:15), 4.17.40. Caught as he is in Augustine's trap of predestination, Calvin cannot see he has lost sight of the graciousness of God and the notion of sacrament as medicine. In regard to baptism, however, adults without faith or children of non-believers receive only an empty sign, 4.16.20. Yet is this not, for Calvin, tantamount to death? At the very least, they are "chargeable" before God, 4.15.15, 17; 4.16.24, 4.17.33, 34.
59. 4.17.40. Such a confession might be appropriate from adult baptizands, but Calvin distinguishes between that and the required examination for the supper, 4.16.24, 31(2).
60. 4.1.15, 4.12.5. See also 3.4.13.

61. 4.1.15, 4.12.4, emphasis mine. Calvin distinguishes between public sin, secret sin, and the intermediate kind about which only one or two others may know, 4.12.3, 6. Serious public sinners are excommunicated; those guilty of the intermediate kind are if they refuse to repent.

62. Hughes Oliphant Old, *The Patristic Roots of Reformed Worship*. Zürich: Theologischer Verlag, 1975, p. 71, 273, 94-95. This would seem to me to demand both more frequent table celebration and ready access to God's healing, nurturing gifts, rather than a fencing of the table.

63. *Grace and Gratitude*, p. 190.

64. 4.10.28-30, 32. Bouwsma understands decorum as moderation, p. 91, 194, as a fitting accommodation, p. 116-7, 124-5, 232.

65. 4.1.1, 4.3.6, 4.15.20-22, 4.17.43.

56. 4.10.14.

67. 4.15.19.

68. 3.4.12, 13, 3.19.8, 4.10.1, 16, 20, 27, 28.

69. 4.17.43.

70. 4.10.29-32.

71. 4.13.14, 4.14.19, 4.15.15, 4.17.38, 4.18.7, 8.

72. 4.17.3, emphasis mine.

73. 4.18.7, 4.10.5, 4.18.1ff.

74. I am indebted to Don Saliers for first expressing this notion in this way.

75. Calvin uses the word *eucharistia* and its cognate *eucharistikon* only eight times in the *Institutes*: 4.14.22 (OS V, p. 280), 4.17.28, citing Augustine (OS V, p. 381), 4.17.48, citing Chrysostom (OS 5, p. 415), 4.18.12 (OS V, p. 427), 4.18.13, 16 in consideration of the nature of sacrifice in general but not as a term for the supper (OS V, p. 429, 431), 4.19.3 (OS V, p. 437), and 4.19.16 (OS V, p. 450). *Eucharistia* is found twice in the preface, p. 20 (OS III, p. 19, 20).

76. 4.14.19, emphasis mine; 4.13.6, 4.14.13, 4.15.1, 4.15.13. We should praise God verbally for what "our faith recognizes in the Sacrament," 4.17.37.

77. 4.17.38, 4.17.1ff, 37.

78. 4.17.38, 44.

79. 4.14.17, 4.14.7.

80. 4.14.18, 4.16.1, 4.17.39, etc. "...nothing more preposterous could happen in the Supper than for it to be turned into a silent action...," 4. 17.39; so also with baptism!

81. 4.14.1, 4.17.11, 4.19.7, etc.

82. 4.17.39, 4.14.4

83. Gerrish asserts the same in *Grace and Gratitude*, p. 85.

84. 4.14.4. This is not to say that persons must be able to comprehend preaching before baptism. See Calvin's arguments regarding infant baptism, 4.16.1ff, and below.

85. 4.15.2.

86. Herein lies Calvin's problem with the Roman church: "Instead of the ministry of the Word, a perverse government compounded of lies rules there....The foulest sacrilege has been introduced in place of the Lord's supper. The worship of God has been deformed by a diverse and unbearable mass of superstitions," 4.2.2.

87. 4.17.33.

88. 4.16.19.

89. 4.14.3. "It is not, therefore, the chief function of the Sacrament simply and without higher consideration to extend to us the body of Christ. Rather, it is to seal and confirm that promise...," 4.17.4.

90. Sacraments represent the promises "as painted in a picture from life," 4.14.5, but it is not enough to look. Participating, eating and drinking are required, 4.17.1, etc.

91. Gerrish affirms this in *Grace and Gratitude,* p. 85.

92. 4.14.14.

93. 4.17.42.

94. 4.17.9, *Catechism*, 132.

95. 4.15.2, 20, 22. Calvin interprets Mark 16.16 to mean that baptism is subordinate to preaching, 4.16.28. But see 4.16.17, 25, where Calvin argues on behalf of infant baptism on the grounds that Christ is life, and the only way to have life is to be engrafted to Christ, and that means baptism.

96. 4.15.3, 4, 4.16.22, 31(9).

97. 4.17.44 and above.

98. 4.17.46. Everyone should receive both elements, since that is what was commanded and exemplified, and because Christ is both food and drink, 4.17.47-50, 4.18.8. Not to do so condemns one as wicked and shameless, to use Chrysostom's words, and invalidates one's prayer, 4.17.45.

99. 4.16.31(9), 4.16.30, and above.

100. 4.18.6, 4.15.3, 4.

101. 4.1.7.

102. 4.1.20, 4.10.20, 4.14.24, 4.15.1, 3, 4.16.4.

103. 4.13.6. Again, this applies to adult baptism only. Infants presumably can make this vow only when they have come to some degree of intentionality, and in Calvin's schema that may well be in their first participation in the supper.

104. 4.15.5, 6, 11, 12, 4.16.2, 3, 17, 18, 30, 31.

105. The supper is a spiritual banquet, 4.17.1, 10. it reminds us that Christ is the bread of life, 4.17.5, the supper is God's way of spiritually feeding the household, 4.18.19, etc.

106. 1.10.2.

107. 3.6.3.

V

WORSHIP AS OUR RECOGNITION OF AND PARTICIPATION IN GOD'S GRACIOUSNESS

> What, therefore, now remains for man, bare and
> destitute of all glory, but to recognize God for
> whose beneficence he could not be grateful
> when he abounded with the riches of God's
> grace; and at least, by confessing his own pov-
> erty, to glorify God in whom he did not previ-
> ously glory in recognition of his own bless-
> ings?[1]

Holistic Worship

We have now seen how Calvin works in a holistic
manner, naming polarities that he then weaves together into
a dynamic whole. Throughout the entirety of the *Institutes*,
this phenomenon recurs. Perhaps we can say that Calvin
bridges a paradigm gap, experiencing within himself the
pros and cons, the pluses and minuses, the fear and the delight, the humility and the glory, the despair and the absolute conviction.[2] Perhaps he simply has not learned the skill
of compartmentalizing dimensions of his life, of tucking
notions and experiences into water-tight compartments that
can be moved around like so much furniture in the theological room of the brain. But no, he clearly manifests the ex-
pertise of the scholastic. Surely he finds such constructed
neatness inimical to his experience, and, given the fact that
the *Institutes* remained under construction for some twenty
years, we may well conclude that his interplay of interests

and issues to present a single, holistic picture is quite intentional.[3] Examples of this holism may be the fact that in the *Institutes*, Calvin's Latin terminology of worship remains essentially consistent throughout. Although occasionally he uses a form of *adorare* or *honorare*, he prefers a form of *colere/cultus*.[4] He applies this cognate cluster elastically, and includes very different kinds of components in that use. But, in complete concordance with the dialogue we have already seen at work in Calvin's theology, he interrelates these components fully. One result of this linguistic consistency is that there can be no real separation of Calvin's address of worship *"passim"* in the *Institutes* from that of prayer, word, sacrament. Nor can we consider ceremonies, for example, as separate from prayer, public or private. Perhaps more importantly, Calvin does not distinguish linguistically between worship as God's act, and worship as ours. So we are compelled to do so as we have, pointing out where God's action is primary, and where what we do somehow contributes to the worship event.

Calvin does attend to worship in three distinct ways. We have already considered his intentional focus on preaching, baptism, and the supper. Secondly, he speaks of worship as he wends his way through discussions of God as creator and provider, through discourses on redemption, justification, sanctification, ecclesiology, and civil law. Although Calvin seems to refer to worship in a passing fashion in these discussions, in each place he has something of interest to tell us that points us along a kind of trajectory towards the larger portrait of what it means to engage in worship with God. We shall see also that he does not come only incidentally to a thorough-going exposition of Christ's prayer, for example, the final type of consideration of worship. All three of these types of attention to worship, along with the content of each type, are inseparable partners. None stands outside the path of explicating the terms of the dialogical relationship between humans and God. True, the weaving is not without a certain irregularity of texture. Nevertheless, we will see again polarities inextricably

linked to each other and to God's graciousness toward us—
dynamic polarities that are paradigmatic of the dialogical
relationship between God and humankind. In any case, Calvin most certainly does not address worship atomistically.
We make a serious mistake if we believe we can focus our
attention solely on Book IV, as we did in the last chapter.
Calvin's consideration of worship in the earlier parts of the
opus is *not* casual, but an intrinsic part of the weaving of
the entirety of the *Institutes*. Unfortunately, by virtue of our
limited capacity, we must address the various aspects of
worship *ad seriatim*, even as we struggle to keep before us
the fact that each aspect we consider breathes life into every other and receives its life from the others.

Honoring God with Affection

With that in mind, let us now consider Calvin's references to right worship as our recognition of and participation in relationship with God. In the *Institutes*, in explication of the first commandment, Calvin writes:

> (God) commands us to worship (*coli*) and adore
> (*adorari*) him with true and zealous godli-
> ness....Even though there are innumerable
> things that we owe to God, yet they may be con-
> veniently grouped in four headings: (1) adora-
> tion (to which is added as an appendix, spiritual
> obedience of the conscience), (2) trust, (3) invo-
> cation, (4) thanksgiving. (1) "Adoration" I call
> the veneration and worship (*cultum*) that each
> of us, in submitting to his greatness, renders to
> him. For this reason, I justly consider as a part
> of adoration the fact that we submit our con-
> sciences to (God's) law. (2) "Trust" is the assu-
> rance of reposing in him that arises from the
> recognition of his attributes, when—attributing
> to him all wisdom, righteousness, might, truth,
> and goodness, we judge that we are blessed
> only by communion with him. (3) "Invocation"
> is that habit of our mind, whenever necessity
> presses us, of resorting to his faithfulness and
> help as our only support. (4) "Thanksgiving" is

> that gratitude with which we ascribe praise to
> him for all good things. As the Lord suffers
> nothing of these to be transferred to another, so
> he commands that all be rendered wholly to
> himself.[5]

In the Geneva Catechism, Calvin provides a more precise,
clear and orderly view of worship:

> M: What is the right way of honoring
>   (God)?
> C: To put all our trust in him; to study to
>   worship him all our life, by obeying his
>   will; to call upon him whenever any
>   need impels us, seeking in him salvation
>   and whatever good things can be de-
>   sired; and lastly, to acknowledge him
>   with both heart and mouth to be the only
>   author of all good things.[6]

Both descriptions offer a definition of worship as
our recognition of God, relational recognition that includes
trust, obedience, invocation, and thanksgiving. For Calvin,
each of these surely is in the first place "properly an emotion of the heart."[7] True worship arises from the inside out,
from feelings, inclinations, affections that rest at the depths
of our being. When we have recognized the greatness of
God and our wretchedness through the spectacles of scripture, Calvin believes we are first moved to fear. But with
the knowledge of and encounter with Christ, and in understanding through the word embodied in preaching and
events at table and font that we are adopted as God's be-
loved children, we perceive that God is truly God *pro nobis*. Thus God enables us not only to be awed by the extent
of God's astonishing graciousness, but also to place our
trust in it as the source and sustenance of our life.[8]

We may well stand in fear of God's judgment, but it
is not, finally, fear alone or even primarily that Calvin wishes to endorse as our motivation for being *pro Deo*. Rather,
"...the beginning of honoring God aright is trust in his mercy,"[9] says Calvin, even though for him fear remains part of

a healthy reverence.[10] Of course, he doesn't speak simply of an intellectual comprehension of God's goodness,[11] but of an embrace of it at the core of our being. So also he is not talking about a surface trust, a limited trust, a partial trust, but about an absolute surrender of the self to the gifts of God. So Calvin can say:

> For in the first place, (God) everywhere commends integrity as the chief part of worshipping him. By this word he means a sincere simplicity of mind, free from guile and feigning, the opposite of a double heart. It is as if it were said that the beginning of right living is spiritual, where the inner feeling of the mind is unfeignedly dedicated to God for the cultivation of holiness and righteousness.[12]

Hypocrites, we know, need not apply,[13] nor the proud. Authentic surrender to God automatically implies humility as "an unfeigned submission of our heart, stricken down in earnest with an awareness of its own misery and want."[14] Such surrender is a constitutional expectation of worship. Thus Calvin proposes the following as rules of prayer:

1. …that we be disposed in mind and heart as befits those who enter conversation with God.[15]
2. …that in our petitions we ever sense our own insufficiency, and earnestly pondering how we need all that we seek, join with this prayer an earnest—nay, burning—desire to attain it.[16]
3. …that anyone who stands before God to pray, in his humility giving glory completely to God, abandon all thought of his own glory, cast off all notion of his own worth, *in fine*, put away all self-assurance—lest if we claim for ourselves anything, even the least bit, we should become vainly puffed up, and perish at his presence.[17]
4. …that, thus cast down and overcome by true humility, we should be nonetheless encour-

aged to pray by a sure hope that our prayer will
be answered.[18]

Yet in a sense trust, humility, integrity only signal a deeper,
richer emotion: gratitude. It is gratitude that God's endless
gifts should evoke; it is gratitude that honors God by af-
firming God as the wellspring of all the life that blesses us
so abundantly and constantly; it is gratitude that should be
our constant attitude and motivation for all our being and
doing.[19]
        Ingratitude offends God. It is contrary to right wor-
ship, and consequently equivalent to idolatry. Gratitude is
inseparable from love for God, since God is *in se* love and
Christ expresses that love *par excellence*. God's love for us
is the ultimate source of our gratitude, and gratitude in turn
begets love. How appropriate, then, that

> we are bidden "to love God with all our heart,
> with all our soul, and with all our faculties."
> Since all the capacities of our soul ought to be
> so filled with the love of God, it is certain that
> this precept is not fulfilled by those who can ei-
> ther retain in the heart a slight inclination or ad-
> mit to the mind any thought at all that would
> lead them away from the love of God into vani-
> ty.[20]

Worship as our activity rests upon these linked affections of the heart. Forgiven, adopted, nurtured, we are
immensely humbled, yet know we are loved because we
experience the divine embrace. We know, too, that the love
deserves trust, gratitude and love in return, not in any partial measure, but wholly and without any reservation whatsoever. These affections, with all the integrity we can mus-
ter, constitute our first expression of worship, and give rise
to every additional expression. But worship does not stop
with affection, any more than love for partner, family or
friend remains internal.

Obedience

Gratitude and trust, generated by love, should, as far as Calvin is concerned, generate obedience. In the first place, "no one gives himself freely and willingly to God's service unless, having tasted his fatherly love, he is drawn to love and worship him in return."[21] Having savored the extraordinary flavor of God's being-for-us, how could one *not* willingly surrender to either the gifts or the call for service— that is, to the Giver? Certainly if our hearts are not filled with love of God, then our activity in worship has no value.[22] But if we wholly engage with such love, active obedience will issue forth.

Among Calvin's many "passing" references to worship, we notice this emphasis on obedience in terms of both internal surrender to God's will and external behavior. In fact, obedience functions at the very least as an enduring pedal-point throughout, whether the discussion specifically addresses the law, prayer, ceremony, or any other issue. But most important is the fact that "lawful worship consists in obedience alone."[23] This obedience manifests itself in "the observance of righteousness, holiness, and purity."[24] Appropriately, Calvin asserts the continuance of the law, not because obedience to the law justifies, for we are justified by God in Christ alone.[25] Rather, we willingly render obedience to the law as eucharistic response to justification. It is the means by which we voluntarily surrender wholly to God's will and live out lives in dialogue with God, lives that are a "practice of godliness,"[26] lives that are, in fact, worship. Obedience is inseparable from faith, for without it none of our works has any value at all, since human beings are incapable of doing any good apart from the good that God does in us.[27]

Obedience serves as the antidote and the prophylactic for idolatry, since focusing all our attentions either directly or indirectly on God leaves no room for focusing anywhere else. We recall that neither the carefully designed colors, aromas or shapes of nature, nor the songs of whales,

birds or crickets schools us adequately in relationship with
God. Not surprisingly, "the custom of the city or the agreement of tradition"[28] will come up abysmally short in making available the information needed for us to worship God
aright. As always, on account of our limited capacity and
our perversity,

> the Lord has provided us with a written law to
> give us a clearer witness of what was too ob-
> scure in the natural law, shake off our listless-
> ness, and strike more vigorously our mind and
> memory.[29]

The Law as Guide

Authentic worship is most certainly prescribed in
the law.[30] Without God's gracious accommodation to us in
the law, while we might be moved to worship, we simply
would not know how to worship. Our ignorance would not
only leave us out of dialogue with God with whom we must
be in lively relationship to be truly human, it carries us
even farther into the realm of defect.[31] Not knowing how to
worship inevitably leads to idolatry, for we are turned by
our lack of knowledge everywhere but where we must
face.[32] God has given us the Decalogue to steer us aright,
and indeed, it may be thought of as a textbook for right
worship.

The first table of the Decalogue speaks of our direct
address of God. In it we learn in no uncertain terms to
whom obedient worship is due, and that the One we are to
adore accepts no superstitious activities or things. This includes the sacrificial worship of the Old Testament as well
as the human construction of the mass, because lawful worship is spiritual worship.[33] We learn that

> whatever our mind conceives of God, whatever
> our tongue utters, should savor of his excel-
> lence, match the loftiness of his sacred name,
> and lastly, serve to glorify his greatness.[34]

We are reminded, then, that the "things" of bread, nectar,

and water are indeed spiritual things. Surely they fulfill the criteria of excellence, loftiness and glorification.

It seems that Calvin perceives this "savoring of God's excellence" to be relatively simple and straight forward. In contrast, idolatry is multivalent in its expression, to say nothing of its deceptiveness. Even though Calvin believes all people "have a vague general veneration for God," few honor God. Most worship a figment of their own imagination, out of presumption, confusion, dullness or perversion.[35]

Thousands of locations solicit our affection, but human beings are much inclined to worship other creatures. Angels or other persons, especially saints, seem to have a particular attraction for us, either claiming our devotion or inviting us to attempt to worship God through them. Either "site" is simply unacceptable, even with the best of intentions.[36] Every shred and shadow of reverence, every syllable of address, belongs only to God: "Nothing," says Calvin, "however slight, can be credited to man without depriving God of his honor, and without man himself falling into ruin through brazen confidence."[37] That indicates that one kind of idolatry is pride, in the self or in any of our kind. Idolatry also includes attributing any form to God, whether it be via sign, painting, or sculpture, lest we in our stupidity come to identify the physical thing with God or any part of God.[38]

Now, Calvin is not an irascible iconoclast bent on stripping every church of every symbol or art. God does, after all, reveal the divine self in signs, and artistic talent and the spiritually faithful works it produces are God-given. Yet adoring the sacramental elements fits the category of idolatry, "for what is idolatry if not this: to worship the gifts in place of the Giver...?"[39] God's incomprehensible reality is not located in things and is not imaginable in things. While physical realities of nature and even the human body may mirror God for us and so make God knowable in some degree to us, it is one thing to worship the God

mirrored, and another, idolatrous, thing to worship the mirror.

The first table of the law also teaches us that God
wants us to root our daily activities in, and permeate them
with, contemplation of God's works.[40] Being open to God
and honoring God remain in the realm of impossibility if
we focus all our time and energy on what we are doing.
How could our lives conform to God's gracious way if we
never take time to stop and consider it, to be informed by it,
to be reshaped by it? Alas, "there is nothing that we are
more unwilling to do than to bid farewell to our own labors
and to give God's works their rightful place."[41] Yet if we
think only upon ourselves, if we attend only to our interests, we have already learned, we are bound to drown in our
own mire.

Prayer

Again God considers our need. As companions to
our worship of trust and obedience, as parallels to the institution of the law, God provides for us another particular
means of assuring our true humanity, our true life as dialogue with God: prayer.

> ...as soon as the law prescribes what we are to
> do, it teaches that the power to obey comes
> from God's goodness. It thus summons us to
> prayers by which we may implore that this pow-
> er be given us. If there were only a command
> and no promise, our strength would have to be
> trusted whether it is sufficient to respond to the
> command. But since with the command are at
> once connected promises that proclaim not only
> that our support, but our whole virtue as well,
> rests in the help of divine grace, they more than
> sufficiently demonstrate how utterly inept, not
> to say unequal, we are to observe the law. [42]

Calvin has claimed obedience as the only acceptable worship. Now he declares that prayer is the chief part of
worship.[43] God ordains that we pray, promises to be access-

ible to us through prayer, and assures us that our prayers
will generate positive results.[44] We can trust this since the
very desire to pray rises in us as a result of God's work
within, and not from our own will.[45] How else would anyone have the courage or motivation to pray, even in the face
of overwhelming need? Similarly, could anyone pray if
one's prayers depended upon one's worth, or on the perfection of one's praying? As our salvation so depends on
God's absolute graciousness, so also does our prayer, "for
God, as has been seen above, declaring that he will be gentle and kind to all, gives to the utterly miserable hope that
they will get what they have sought."[46]

God will respond to an earnest heart, even if our
prayer is ragged around the edges or downright inept. Rhetorical skill is not the measure here, but reverence, sinceri-
ty, penitence, humility and "confident hope" are.[47] Of
course we ought to pray to the best of our ability, for that
inheres in true reverence according to Calvin's explication
of the first part of the law. Calvin counsels careful focusing
of all our resources in prayer, lest our thoughts, feelings
and energies stray and scatter like fall leaves in a whimsical
wind.[48] Even so, the most reverent and attentive praying
will not render our prayer acceptable before God or ensure
God's presence and favor in response to our invocation.
No, only Christ can do that, and so right prayer calls on
God in the name of Christ. Not surprisingly, Calvin supports this claim with the affirmation that Christ is the sole
mediator and intercessor on our behalf before God, in
prayer and in everything else. Prayer to or through any other is a clear cut case of idolatry.[49]

Still, do we not know how to pray at all? As we had
so much difficulty recognizing God-*pro-nobis* do we continue muddled, lost and resistant when it comes to prayer?
Does our courage fail us at the very idea or when it comes
to the moment of direct conversation with the Divine?
Here, too, God meets our fragility and incorrigibility with
continuing accommodation. We need only to look at Scripture which encourages us in prayer, advises us how and for

what to pray. Scripture offers many forms of prayer to aid
us, and we are urged to engage in entreaties and supplica-
tions linked with thanksgivings. If there is no scriptural
promise of what we seek, we should pray conditionally, although Calvin insists that we not pray for the dead.[50]

A Model for Prayer

Scripture does offer one model Calvin considers so
excellent he insists it will never fail us. Just as Christ was
God's accommodation *par excellence* in regard to our identity, so God gives us a similar gift in regard to prayer: that
which has been deemed Jesus' own:

> since (God) saw that we did not even sufficient-
> ly perceive how straitened our poverty was,
> what it was fair to request, and what was profit-
> able for us, he also provided for this ignorance
> of ours; and what had been lacking to our ca-
> pacity he supplied and made sufficient from his
> own. For he prescribed a form for us in which
> he set forth as in a table all that he allows us to
> seek of him, all that is of benefit to us, all that
> we need ask. From this kindness of his we re-
> ceive great fruit of consolation: that we know
> we are requesting nothing absurd, nothing
> strange or unseemly—in short, nothing unac-
> ceptable to him—since we are asking almost in
> his own words.[51]

Notice Calvin says "almost" God's own words. Herein he
intimates three points: (1) that the prayer, as the rest of
scripture, does not present verbatim the Word of God; (2)
that whatever holiness accrues to the prayer does not accrue
to the prayer *in se* but to the one to whom it points, and
therefore it is not to be made an object of veneration; (3)
that the prayer is a model, and not the only acceptable
prayer.[52] Jesus' prayer teaches not a requisite form or set of
words, but a basic content. This content reflects God's glory as well as the fundamental dialogical relationship between us and God.[53] By addressing God parentally, we ac-

claim God's infinite love toward us and our homage in response.[54] At the same time, the claim is made that our humanity is determined not solely in relationship with God, but also with regard to our sisters and brothers. It is, after all, *our* Parent we address, and all our blessings are shared. Thus all prayer has to do with the neighbor as much as with God.[55] Meanwhile we recognize the appropriateness of praising God, for in God alone we can find all that is ultimately good, right and valuable, and our praise attests our surrender to the gracious divine will. Even by asking for all that we need for life, we extol the wonderful love of God, acknowledging both our authentic needs and our incapacity to meet them. Especially among these is our own continual failure to love God and neighbor.[56]

Even with all this, we still really have little capacity to pray aright, and so once more God's gracious accommodation takes an active role. God provides us with the Spirit as "our teacher in prayer."[57] Even if one cannot read, learn or comprehend Christ's prayer, or fashion a prayer that coherently addresses one's need and God's graciousness, God still can receive the deepest cries of the heart. The Spirit serves here as the dynamic link that gathers the participants together in intimate relationship.

Benefits of Prayer

So, there can be no mistaking that prayer, even petition, glorifies God as part of our worshipful address to God. At the same time, it also serves those who pray. Prayer is a means of accessing God's goodness toward us, for "we dig up by prayer the treasures that were pointed out by the Lord's gospel, and which our faith has gazed upon."[58] That same faith is essential for prayer. Without faith, prayer receives nothing, for faith alone grasps the promises of God. Faith gives birth to prayer, faith guides prayer, and God finds acceptable only such faithful prayer.[59] But if God gifts us with faith, then, do we need anything else for life? Certainly, for even God-given faith cannot be sustained by us apart from the nourishment provided through prayer. More-

over, whether or not we are aware of any need, God invites
us to prayer, and the benefits are rich indeed:

> Therefore, even though, while we grow dull and
> stupid toward our miseries, (God) watches and
> keeps guard on our behalf, and sometimes even
> helps us unasked, still it is very important for us
> to call upon him: First, that our hearts may be
> fired with a zealous and burning desire ever to
> seek, love, and serve him, while we become ac-
> customed in every need to flee to him as to a sa-
> cred anchor. Secondly, that there may enter our
> hearts no desire and no wish at all of which we
> should be ashamed to make a witness, while we
> learn to set all our wishes before his eyes, and
> even to pour out our whole hearts. Thirdly, that
> we be prepared to receive his benefits with true
> gratitude (*gratitudine*) of heart and thanksgiving
> (*gratiarum*), benefits that our prayer reminds us
> come from his hand. Fourthly, moreover, that,
> having obtained what we were seeking, and be-
> ing convinced that he has answered our prayers,
> we should be led to meditate upon his kindness
> more ardently. And fifthly, that at the same time
> we embrace with greater delight those things
> which we acknowledge to have been obtained
> by prayers. Finally, that use and experience may
> according to the measure of our feebleness, con-
> firm his providence, while we understand not
> only that he promises never to fail us, and of his
> own will opens the way to call upon him at the
> very point of necessity, but also that he ever ex-
> tends his hand to help his own, not wet-nursing
> them with words but defending them with
> present help.[60]

Prayer functions as a microcosm of the dialogue of
relationship: in our trusting, grateful, obedient prayer we
fittingly worship God. At the same time God accommodates to our realities and meets our needs, first by giving us
prayer, then by responding to it. Both we and God are enlivened and enriched (although Calvin, finding all perfection in God would be more inclined to say that God is
pleased). Such prayer, subjectively speaking, ought to be

ceaseless if for no other reason than that God desires it, but also because our needs are constant and because God's care of us is constant. In addition, we are true temples of prayer, and ought to live out our function. Obviously Calvin maintains no interest in prayer-ritual for its own sake, nor in once-in-awhile prayer. He instead intends a disciplined exercise of the synapses, muscles and joints of relationship.[61]

The Day of Assembly

The third commandment also commends to us another means of such exercise, that of the public assembly. God sets apart a day a week for us to recall God's own graciousness and to give us rest from our self-wearying,

> ...and from our everyday experience we well know how we need them. But how can such meetings be held unless they have been established and have their stated days? According to the apostle's statement, "all things should be done decently and in order" among us. It is so impossible to maintain decency and order — otherwise than by this arrangement and regulation —that immediate confusion and ruin threaten the church if it be dissolved.... For our most provident and merciful Father willed to see our needs not less than those of the Jews.[62]

For us not to observe the day is self-destructive behavior. To observe it as a ritual holy unto itself engages us in idolatry. It is not the specific day *in se* that matters. Of course, Saturday as the Jewish Sabbath has been furfilled in Christ, and Sunday is most appropriate because the Jewish Sabbath is fulfilled precisely in the resurrection. Why not every day?

> If only this had been given us! Spiritual wisdom truly deserved to have some portion of time set apart for it each day. But if the weakness of many made it impossible for daily meetings to be held, and the rule of love does not allow more to be required of them, why should we not

> obey the order we see laid upon us by God's
> will?[63]

This does not preclude more frequent meetings if appropriate, but a definite day is necessary "as a remedy needed to keep order in the church."[64] Moreover, human incapacity renders us ill equipped to offer God rightful worship without the aid of the gathered family of God and the events that occur in that community. Consequently, we have commended to us regular public assembly, wherein we might be helped in our recognition of God. Indeed, a part of our obedience is that we "observe together the lawful order set by the church for the hearing of the Word, the administration of the sacraments, and for public prayers."[65]

Calvin intentionally chooses this word order to demonstrate his own obedience. For the same reason we examined preaching, bath and supper in advance of this chapter. We also recall that it is in public assembly that we are virtually guaranteed access to the gifts of God by which we know the transcendent one is immanently *pro nobis* always. Nonetheless, we find public prayer to be of significant import. It is ordained by God, and is not to be scorned, for

> whoever refused to pray in the holy assembly of
> the godly knows not what it is to pray individu-
> ally, or in a secret spot, or at home. Again, he
> who neglects to pray alone and in private, how-
> ever unremittingly he may frequent public as-
> semblies, there contrives only windy prayers
> ....[66]

In fact, while all other aspects of prayer already noted continue appropriate in public prayer, now there is an additional concern: edification. What would be more useless than public prayer that does not empower partners in dialogue to communicate with each other? That does not help participants know one another better, that does not enable and enrich loving and faithful relationship? So public prayer ought to be in the language of the people, clear, coherent, understandable. That necessarily excludes flamboyant language that only serves to confuse and to foster pride.[67] Yes, Calvin is a skilled orator, but as his sermons and commentaries evidence, rhetoric *serves* gospel. Moreover, a skilled orator knows how to use clear, coherent, and understandable language!

Calvin also urges public confession of sin, for through it, "a gate to prayer is opened both to individuals in private and to all in public."[68] Confession is essential precisely because the sin of pride so readily permeates us. Rather than clinging to the humility Calvin promotes, we would much prefer to flatter ourselves by emphasizing our good qualities and behavior and de-emphasizing, even ignoring, our less than acceptable side. To do so courts disaster and ruin, since pride and arrogance turn us away from God and into idolatry. Thus confession must certainly serve to remind us not only of our own miserable state, but also of God's amazing graciousness.[69] Lest we plummet into despair over our condition, and as a firm assertion of God's love and thus our imputed worth, Calvin strongly endorses public declaration of pardon:

> For when the whole church stands, as it were, before God's judgment seat, confesses itself guilty, and has its sole refuge in God's mercy, it is no common or light solace to have present there the ambassador of Christ, armed with the mandate of reconciliation, by whom it hears proclaimed its absolution.[70]

Alas, Calvin apparently never managed to convince the Genevan worthies of the value of the declaration of pardon.[71] One can only wonder how many good Christians were left tottering on the edge of despair, unsure whether or not they were among those who ought to be included in the soon to occur excommunication.

Along with prayer and confession, the recitation of the Apostles' Creed is suitable, for it provides a most helpful summary of Christian belief and "may serve as a tablet for us upon which we see distinctly and point by point the things in Christ that we ought to heed."[72] As well, while Calvin unquestionably believes the human voice is most appropriately put to use in public prayer, he does not dispute the value of singing, since "we know by experience that singing has great power and vigor to move and inflame men's hearts to call upon and praise God with a more vehement and burning zeal.[73] As with all the arts, God can readily be seen as the author of music, and in God is found all real cause for singing.[74] But music also has a teaching function. Consequently, the text matters most, not the tune.[75] It is hardly any wonder, then, that Calvin would find the psalms the most suitable texts for singing.

Ceremonies

Calvin speaks often of ceremonies (*ceremonarium*). In Christ, ceremonies of the Old Testament are rescinded in use, although their sign value is still in effect.[76] As scriptural content they still point to the benefits incarnate in Christ, but the ceremonies of the New Testament have replaced those of the Old in use. The foremost of these, supper and baptism, we have already examined. The laying on of hands in ordination and blessing may also count as a sacrament, although Calvin remains ambivalent about this.[77] The primary value of all ceremonies is that they witness to and present Christ and Christ's benefits.[78] At the same time, ceremonies exercise faith. Indeed, all of worship is a function, profession and exercise of faith![79] Because Calvin believes God has graciously and accommodatingly defined right worship for us, it only stands to reason that he also believes creating our own worship without regard for scripture qualifies as idolatry.[80] Carefully attending to Scripture's guidelines serves as a life raft in a sea of potential "vicious rites."[81] In fact, he bluntly says: "In short, every chance invention, by which men seek to worship God, is nothing but a pollution of true holiness."[82] Still, we are not rigidly bound to unbending rubrics, because God

> did not will in outward discipline and ceremo-
> nies to prescribe in detail what we ought to do
> (because he foresaw that this depended upon the
> state of the times, and he did not deem one form
> suitable for all ages)....[83]

God accommodates the divine self according to our realities, recognizing that what suits one part of the family at one time and place may not suit another part elsewhere and else when. As the content and context of our life changes, faithful worship also changes, witnessing anew to God's tender, accommodating love by adjusting to our new reality. How are we to know, then, what ceremonies are authentic? Calvin does not leave us to our own devices. First and foremost, we are to attend carefully to God's Word, and add nothing to it.[84] The governance of the Word, if we attend to it carefully, will ensure that any ceremonies we do show Christ, as they must. Beyond that, Calvin helps us a little more with what is acceptable in honoring God. In harmony with right public prayer and song, any ceremony is rejected if it is not useful. Ceremonies should certainly edify. We need to understand what we are doing as best we can, so that we can communicate as fully as possible. Superstition is precluded, as we have earlier seen, as is ceremonial, physical sacrifice such as that practiced in Old Testament times and that presumed to occur in the mass. God is to be worshipped spiritually, Calvin's exposition of the Decalogue tells us. That may entail use of the physical elements recognized by scripture, but any attempt to "sew innumerable patches"[85] on the death on the cross trivializes and obscures that once-for-all-time event. Moreover, ostentation, pomp, extravagance is wholly inappropriate because such does not edify or aid in the conversation. Rather, such displays confuse and befuddle worshippers, and ignorance and confusion lead to sacrilege.[86]

In addition to public assembly as a whole with its proclamation of Word, celebration of baptism and the supper, almsgiving and prayer are cited by Calvin as the "unvarying rule" for the church.[87] Now Calvin's order for worship does not always mention almsgiving.[88] However, in Calvin's essay "Du Sacrament de la Cène," included in some editions of the *Church Prayers*, Calvin develops this theme:

> For, aroused and moved by the reading and explanation of the gospel and the confession of our faith, which is done just before, we ponder in memory that Jesus Christ is given to us of the infinite goodness of the heavenly Father and with him all things, i.e., the remission of sins, the covenant of eternal salvation, the life and righteousness of God, and finally, all desirable things which are added unto the children of God, i.e., to those who seek his kingdom and his righteousness. Then with good and just cause, we offer and submit ourselves completely to God the Father and to our Lord Jesus Christ, in recognition of so many and so great benefits. And (as Christian love [*charitè*] requires) we testify this by holy offerings and gifts which are administered to Jesus Christ in his least ones, i.e., those who are hungry, thirsty, naked, a stranger, sick, or held in prison. For all who live in Christ, and have him dwelling in them do voluntarily what the law commands them. And the latter commands that one not appear before God without an offering.[89]

Once again we see the connection between our relationship with God and our relationship with others. Yes, in worship events we experience the richness of God-for-us. Yes, in worship events we recognize God and honor God. But this activity does not and cannot conclude behind the church doors, but has its full and natural expression in all our daily living. What is of God and what is of humankind are inextricably integrated, for the relationality swirls in every different direction at once.

Freedom and Focus

Other ceremonies may be included, if they are instructive and otherwise helpful. Kneeling at prayer, for instance, Calvin accepts, and a burial rite.[90] If there are no mandates and no prohibitions in scripture, we may exercise freedom of conscience (even though, as noted above, we are permitted to add nothing to God's word). We cannot be accused of idolatry or heresy if we choose not to use such behaviors as means of worshipping God.[91] In fact, Calvin frequently rages against the tyranny of imposing on Christians behaviors that are not required in scripture but are claimed to be requisite for salvation.

Even so, we do not possess absolute freedom of conscience in regard to worship. We are not to change old patterns rashly, or innovate whimsically, but accommodatingly. While the end of our worship is the glory of God, we do not arrive there without engagement with other humans. Sensitivity to others' needs and feelings is always in order, and decorum is essential. Above all we must work in the context of love, which "will best judge what may hurt or edify; and if we let love be our guide, all will be safe."[92]

Still, this is not Humanist love. What is absolutely requisite, as we already know, is that all worship be unequivocally *Christian*. For what is Christ if not the quintessential expression of love through whom we know the ultimacy and infinity of God's love? So "no worship has ever pleased God except that which looked to Christ."[93] This is so because in Christ we find our salvation, and

> ...the moment we turn away even slightly from him, our salvation, which rests firmly in him, gradually vanishes away. As a result, those who do not repose in him voluntarily deprive themselves of all grace.[94]

Christ alone redeems, and through Christ we receive forgiveness of sins and all the other benefits God chooses to shower upon us.[95] Christ alone mediates, and is the only priest who can make any effort on our part to worship God acceptable. Indeed, when by God's gracious gift of faith we are bound to Christ, Christ's praise becomes our own.[96] Yet is not such prayer idolatry? Certainly not to Calvin's mind. Such worship is appropriate because Christ shares the di-

vinity of God.[97] So, "we are particularly bidden to call upon
(God) in Christ's name; and we have the promise made that
we shall obtain what we have asked in his name."[98]

Naming Christ as the gateway of prayer, as the way
of worship, we have ready access to our loving, gracious
God:

> Besides, what is better and closer to faith than
> to feel assured that God will be a propitious Fa-
> ther where Christ is recognized as brother and
> propitiator? Then confidently to look for all
> happy and prosperous things from Him whose
> unspeakable love toward us went so far that
> "he...did not spare his own Son but gave him up
> for us all?" (Rom. 8:32) Than to repose in cer-
> tain expectation of salvation and eternal life,
> when we meditate upon Christ, given by the Fa-
> ther, in whom such treasures are hidden?[99]

In Christ, all our uncertainty about divine benevolence toward us evaporates; all anxiety about whether or not God is
for us melts away.

Multi-Dimensional Relatedness

At the same time, our focus on Christ deals not only
with worshipful relationship with God as mapped out by
the first part of the Decalogue. For in Christ we see lived
out as well the worshipful response toward God via the
neighbor:

> ...apart from the fear of God men do not pre-
> serve equity and love among themselves. There-
> fore we call the worship of God the beginning
> and foundation of righteousness. When it is re-
> moved, whatever equity, continence or temper-
> ance men practice among themselves is in
> God's sight empty and worthless. We call it
> source and spirit because from it men learn to
> live with one another in moderation and without
> doing injury, if they honor God as Judge of
> right and wrong. Accordingly, in the First Ta-
> ble, God instructs us in piety and the proper du-

> ties of religion, by which we are to worship his
> majesty. The Second Table prescribes how in
> accordance with the fear of his name we ought
> to conduct ourselves in human society.[100]

We find our true identity and being in relationship with
God, but not apart from relationship with our neighbor.
Worship thus effects our being-in-dialogue in both dimensions—toward God and toward humankind—and integrally
links a series of polarities. Indeed, we can certainly say that
for Calvin, the dialogue between us and God is understood
to be paradigmatic for the relationship between human and
human.

The second table of the law outlines this human-
directed movement forthwith: if we honor and obey God,
we will similarly respect others, for humanity

> is both the image of God, and our flesh. Now, if
> we do not wish to violate the image of God, we
> ought to hold our neighbor sacred. And if we do
> not wish to renounce all humanity, we ought to
> cherish his as our own flesh.[101]

Thus one means of committing idolatry is to fail to treasure
our sibling's life "dear and precious to us," or to fail in
"those duties of love which can apply to its preserva-
tion."[102] This is so whether we are dealing with parents, or
neighbors, or with their possessions. Each person exists in
relationship with provident God, and in every respect, the
way we treat the other ultimately comes home to God.
More, we do not live in a closed community. Our care of
others as siblings or neighbors reaches beyond those whom
we know, even beyond the baptized: "we ought to embrace
the whole human race without exception in a single feeling
of love," says Calvin.[103]

Violation of another (or another's "goods") becomes violation of God. Love of other (and care for others'
living) is a part of loving God, because when we encom-
pass our neighbors and siblings with "all the duties of love"
God is honored.[104]

Calvin's commendation that we worship corporately references this inter-relationality. We are members of the body of Christ. As adopted children we belong to the family of faith, and the family needs to gather in order to relate lovingly with one another. So God calls us to participate in public assembly in which God acts as the center of our human relating together. When the family does gather, the model prayer addresses God parentally, immediately reminding us that we are linked in double relationship with siblings. So also we dare not ask forgiveness from God without also forgiving others in turn. In our prayers we are encouraged to pray for others.[105] Though we are bound to the Word, we have freedom in worship, but not past the limits of what is not only inoffensive to those around us, but is also permeated with and expressive of love. Even excommunication Calvin enjoins for the health and welfare of the community as well as for the individual.

Nevertheless, what is true in public assembly is equally valid in the street, for we are to see all persons as mirroring the image of God. We are whole beings, and therefore are to live whole lives that practice, from a fundamental disposition of the heart, true godliness, piety, worship. What hypocrisy would be ours if we stopped with the clock or the members of the congregation! Our prayer ought to be constant, not only for those we know and love but for the unknown. Almsgiving also remains essential to considering the other our "debtor" and embracing the world in love.[106]

Thus we see Calvin's continued emphasis on dialogical relationship in terms of (1) embracing God's being-in-graciousness for us and our being-in-truth only by virtue of that graciousness, (2) our response to that in honoring God as God desires with our deepest affections, obedience, prayer, and public assembly, and (3) our relationship with God being both expressed and accomplished in relationship with humanity as well. If honoring God means obedience to God, and obedience to God places half its emphasis on behavior toward neighbor, then idolatry is failure to care for the neighbor since such failure indicates we are worshipping someone or something other than God.

What amazing value God sets on humankind in this way, incapacitated, miserable wretches that Calvin sees us to be! God loves us, creates life for us by bringing us into relationship with the divine self. God claims that right response to that gift of love is making the "God-ward" relationship paradigmatic for one directed toward humanity, without which we are not truly human, not truly alive. Of course, all worship ultimately points to God, since we are not to adore gifts or other creatures but the giver. Our final referent is always God. But we cannot get to the final referent without loving referent to neighbor.

> The moral law...is contained under two heads, one of which simply commands us to worship God with pure faith and piety; the other, to embrace men with sincere affection.[107]

Calvin might as well say that right worship, true human life, is so comprised, embracing the polarities of divinity and humanity in a holistic relationship that cannot be broken down into distinct parts without violation of the whole, without sin. Here is another case where the polarities of what is of God and what is of humankind are woven inextricably together into a matrix where distinct strands may remain clearly visible, even as they are equally inseparable.

God remains the prime cause of all this. We cannot worship God aright without the knowledge of the realities with which we deal, knowledge that is provided us by God in incessant aids and helps such as inherent knowledge, scripture, Christ, the Spirit. We cannot worship God aright without God motivating us by God's gifts of loving care, gifts that empower trust and the desire to fulfill the law. We cannot worship God aright without God giving us the law to clarify for us how we can worship authentically. Nor can we worship God aright without participating in that worship privately but also corporately, for there is no other way for us to be *pro Deo* apart from relationship with other human beings. Worship unavoidably is a matter of the whole being, not merely the mind or the tongue or even the heart, but "all members of our body resound (God's) praise in every way they can."[108] Worship is a matter of our whole life, and every phase of it.

Yet again we are dealing with our limitations and God's gracious accommodations. Worship is unquestionably a matter of God being *pro nobis* and of our being *pro Deo*, of our being *pro Deo* precisely by being also *pro* other. It is a matter of the heart and of correspondent active behavior. And it is a matter of *our response* to God's gracious address of us being inseparable, both in terms of motivation and accomplishment, from God's address to us. For everything we do aright in worshipping God, be it in the privacy of our closet at home or in public assembly or in the street, all that we are and do is gift of God.

> ...all the passages that keep occurring in the Scriptures, in which calling upon God is enjoined upon us, are as so many banners set up before our eyes to inspire us with confidence. It would be rashness itself to burst into God's sight if he himself had not anticipated our coming by calling us. Therefore he opens a way for us in his own words: I will say to them, "You are my people...." We see how he precedes those who worship him, and would have them follow him, and thus not to fear for the sweetness of the melody that he himself dictates.[109]

NOTES

1. 2.2.1.

2. See Bouwsma, 230ff, for his final assessment of the composite Calvin.

3. Gerrish notes Calvin "looked assiduously for the interconnections between doctrines...." *Grace and Gratitude*, p 16.

4. 1.11.10, 1.12.3, 1.13.11, 1.14.10, 2.8.22, 4.10.14, 4.18.8, 4.17.37. These uses appear to be random choices. Peter Brunner suggests Calvin quite readily uses *cultus* for worship writ large, but not for

those particular events for which the congregation gathers that embrace both divine and human activity. Here he struggles for new, or more clearly biblical language, language that reflects the intentional, focused coming together of the faithful for dialogical engagement with the divine. Peter Brunner, *Worship in the Name of Jesus*, St. Louis: Concordia Publishing House, 1968, p. 317, note 43. Tr. M.H. Bertram, "Zur Lehre vom Gottesdienst der im Namen Jesu versammelten Gemeinde in Leiturgia," *Handbuch des evangelischen Gottesdienstes*, Vol. 1, Kassel: Johannes Stauda Verlag, 1954, Karl Ferdinand Müller and Walter Blankenburg, eds. The character of worship as seen by Calvin surely indicates this bent, as we shall show, even if the particular language remains less than adequate.

5. 2.8.16. Note that God desires to be worshipped, 1.5.6, 3.16.2.

6. "Catechismus Ecclesiae Genevensis," OS, Vol. II, ¶ 7. See also ¶ 129, 233, 234, 296. "The Catechism of the Church of Geneva, that is, a Plan for Instructing Children in the Doctrine of Christ," in *Calvin: Theological Treatises*, J.K.S. Reid, ed., *The Library of Christian Classics: Ichthus Edition*, Philadelphia: The Westminster Press, 1954, p. 91-92. Note this translator has rendered *colere* as "to serve." See also p. 107, 119-120, 129. In the catechism, the first part of worship leads to an address of the salvation economy; the second, of the law; invocation leads to discussion of prayer; the final part of worship includes the integrated word and sacrament. See also Calvin's *Epistre au Lecteur, La Form Des Prières et Chantz Ecclesiastiques*, OS Vol. ll, 12-18; Tr. F.L. Battles, "John Calvin: The Form of Prayers and Songs of the Church, 1542—Letter to the Reader." *Calvin Theological Joumal*, Vol. 15, No. 2, November, 1980.

7. *Cordis affectum*, 3.20.29, 3.3.16, 3.20.31.

8. 1.10.2.

9. 3.16.3.

10. "let the fear of the Lord be for us a reverence compounded of honor and fear," 3.2.26.

11. 3.2.14-16; see also 1.14.22, 2.8.16, 3.13.3, 3.17.1 and the preface to the *Institutes*, p. 13. It may be correct to say that Calvin makes a quantitative distinction between faith and trust, but it does not appear as if there is a qualitative one.

12. 3.6.5, 3.20.7.

13. "God hates nothing more than counterfeit worship," 4.13.7; 1.4.4, 3.20.7, 4.10.11.

14. 3.12.6, 2.2.11, citing Augustine; 3.20.8, 3.20.11.

15. 3.20.4.

16. 3.20.6.

17. 3.20.8.

18. 3.20.11.

19. 3.20.28. Calvin admits of two types of sacrifice: praise and reverence (*latreutikon et sebastikon*) and thanksgiving (*euxaristikon*),

4.18.13, OS V, p. 429. In the latter "are included all the duties of love....all our prayers, praises, thanksgivings (*gratiarum actiones*), and whatever we do in the worship of God," 4.18.16. This kind of sacrifice "is so necessary for the church that it cannot be absent from it," 4.18.16, OS V, p. 431. Indeed, Gerrish proposes that "...the theme of grace and gratitude...lies at the heart of Calvin's entire theology...." *Grace and Gratitude*, p. 20.

    20. 3.3.11.
    21. 1.5.3.
    22. 3.20.28, 4.18.16.
    23. 2.8.5, 3.2.26, 3.20.14.
    24. 2.8.2. Obedience includes actively fighting against evil, 1.14.15.
    25. 3.11.20, 3.17.1.
    26. 3.19.2.
    27. 2.5.7. Works are worthless without God first purifying, justifying, the worker, 3.14.8, 3.16.1.
    28. 1.5.13.
    29. 2.8.1. In addressing the first table of the law, Calvin says, "What soul, relying upon natural perception, ever had an inkling that the lawful worship of God consists in these and like matters?" 2.2.24.
    30. 1.12.1, 3, 2.2.24, 2.8.1, 2; authentic worship is also prescribed in the gospel, 4.10.8, 30.
    31. If that is indeed possible. We have seen that being out of relationship with God is clearly death.
    32. 1.5.15, 1.11.13
    33. 1.4.3, 1.11.9, 2.7.1, 2.8.8, 13-17, 31, 4.2.2, 4.17.36, 37.
    34. 2.8.22. So also 3.20.41.
    35. 1.2.2, 1.4.1, 1.5.12, 1.5.15
    36. 1.12.1, 3, 1.13.13, 1.14.10, 12, 3.5.3, 3.20.21-25.
    37. 2.2.1, 10, 3.13.1, 2, 3.15.3, 3.20.41.
    38. 1.11.9. See also 1.11.1ff.
    39. 4.17.36, 1.11.3, 12, 4.14.12, 4.17.35, 4.18.8.
    40. 2.8.28-31, 34.
    41. 2.3.9
    42. 2.5.7.
    43. 3.20.29. This has to do specifically with public prayer in the temple—as opposed to sacrifice being the predominant element of worship. But Calvin does not really separate public from private prayer, and rightly so, since prayer is both individual and corporate, and whoever neglects one or the other never truly prays. The Christian worships in prayer, private and corporate, and in obedience, which we shall see is also private and corporate.
    44. 3.20.2, 3, 11-16, 30, 40, 44. Faith, of course, must precede. 3.20.27.
    45. 2.2.27.

46. 3.20.14.

47. 3.20.4-14.

48. 3.20.4-5.

49. 3.5.3, 3.20.21, 27, 4.18.17, etc. The heavenly members of the *"communio sanctorum"* may be engaged in prayer on our behalf, but they are done with earthly cares and it is not given to us to appeal to them, 3.20.24.

50. 3.5.10.

51. 3.20.34.

52. 3.20.49.

53. 3.20.35.

54. 3.20.36, 37, 40.

55. 3.20.38. See also the address of the second table of the Decalogue, below.

56. 3.20.41-46.

57. 3.20.5.

58. 3.20.2, 3.

59. 3.20.27, 11, 14, 51.

60. 3.20.3. Here again we see the weaving: graciousness, trust, obedience, invocation, gratitude.

61. 2.8.34, 3.20.7, 3.20.28, 30.

62. 2.8.32. We have earlier referred to P. Brunner's note regarding Calvin's use of terminology. In the *Institutes* we find such names as "public prayers," 3.20.29 (*publicas orationes*, OS IV, p. 338), "common prayers," 3.20.29 (*communes Ecclesiae preces*, OS IV, p.338), "public assembly," 4.1.5 (*publicos coetus*, OS V, p. 9), "ministry of Word and participation in the mysteries," 4.1.16 (*verbi ministerio, tum sacrorum mysteriorum participationi*, OS V, p. 20-21) "worship," 4.2.2 (*cultus Dei*, OS V, p. 31), "holy assembly," 3.4.11 (*sacro conventu*, OS IV, p. 98) 4.3.10 (*sacro coetu*, OS V, p. 51), "outward communion," 4.1.19 (*externam Ecclesiae communionum*, OS V, p. 23), etc. Calvin often does not make tidy distinctions between personal, individual worship and corporate worship. When it is essential, for example, in regard to the celebration of the supper, he does so, and when he wants to speak particularly to either private or public worship. But apart from that, acceptable prayer is the same whether prayed by one or a whole community; worshiping an image is idolatry whether it is done by one in a closet or by a crowd in a church. What applies to one for the most part applies to the other unless Calvin specifically indicates otherwise.

63. 2.8.32, 33, 34.

64. 2.8.33, 3.20.29.

65. 2.8.34. Calvin notes Psalm 84.2-3 which he interprets as David's despair at being unable to have access to the tabernacle: *"nempe quod fidelibus nihil pluris est hoc adminiculo, quo Deus suos gradatim in sublime attolit."* See also OS V, p. 10; Battles renders this: "believers have no greater help than public worship, for by it God raises his own

folk upward step by step," 4.1.5, 4.1.1.

66. 3.20.29, 30.

67. 3.20.30, 33.

68. 3.4.11. In 4.1.23, Calvin notes that indeed, confession of sin is required of each of us—but it does not have to be public confession.

69. 2.1.2. 3, 2.7.6, 3.3.15.

70. 3.4.14. With regard to discipline, Calvin counsels care that the one disciplined not be "overwhelmed with sorrow," 4.1.29, 4.12.8, 9.

71. Thompson, *Liturgies of the Western Church*, p. 191, 198.

72. 2.16.18, 8.

73. "Epistre du Lecteur," OS II, 15; Battles, "Letter to the Reader," 163.

74. 3.20.29, 31.

75. 3.20.31, 32. Calvin gives inadequate credit to non-textual music to speak in ways no words can. But it must be remembered that he stands amid excessive and perhaps even bizarre applications of music in the mass, ranging from incoherent Latin plainchant to the increasingly polyphonic and extravagant choral and instrumental masses of the High Renaissance, many of which included the use of secular (pub) tunes in sacred compositions. See Jay Grout, *A History of Western Music*. New York: W. W. Norton & Company, Inc. 1960, especially chapters 6-8.

76. 2.7.16, 2.7.17, 2.8.31; see also 2.11.8, 4.14.20-25. In 4.5.5 and 4.10.14, the importation of ceremonies and symbols of Jewish worship is subject to criticism.

77. "Although there exists no set precept for the laying on of hands, because we see it in continual use with the apostles, their very careful observance ought to serve in lieu of a precept....For if the Spirit of God establishes nothing without cause in the church, we should feel that this ceremony, since it has proceeded from him, is not useless, provided it not be turned to superstitious abuse," 4.3.16. Calvin identifies this hand-laying as a sacrament in 4.19.31, but in 4.18.20 claims there is no third sacrament. Hand-laying as a blessing— not a sacrament— when young people affirm their faith Calvin values and wishes restored, 4.19.14, but the apostolic hand-laying that conferred gifts of the Spirit other than those given in baptism is no longer operative, 4.19.6. Hand-laying in healing is *not* now to be done 4.19.18, any more than just because Christ breathed on the disciples does that mean we ought to do so, 4.19.7.

78. This is true also of the Old Testament ceremonies, 2.7.2, 16, 2.11.4, 4.10.14, 15, 29.

79. 1.2.2, 2.2.24, 3.20.31, 4.10.29, 4.14.1, 4.15.1, 13, 4.17.5, 7.

80. 1.4.3, 1.5.13, 1.12.1, 3, 2.8.17, 4.10.8ff.

81. 1.12.1. In 4.20.3 we find that a function of civil law is "the duty of rightly establishing religion." Calvin qualifies that by assuring his readers that this does not mean civil authorities may make their own

rules for worship; they are bound by the definitions God has provided. Calvin's distress with the Roman rites had to do with the fact that Rome mandated participation in elaborate ceremonies that had no basis in God's Word and served only to confuse, 4.10.6ff.

82. 4.10.25.

83. 4. 10.30, 31; 2.11.13. This provides a springboard for the use of worship directories rather than prayer books.

84. 2.1.4, 3.5.10, 4.10.7, 8, 16, 17, 30, 4.13.2, 4.16.1, 4.17.35, 4.18.9. Accordingly, Calvin undermines Roman sacraments other than baptism and the supper—they are not prescribed by God's Word, but they are prescribed by the Roman Church as essential for salvation, 4.19.1ff.

85. 4.18.3.

86. 4.10.12-17, 29, 30, 4.18.1, 3, 12, 13-18.

87. 4.17.44.

88. 2.8.34, 4.17.43, nor does the Form of Church Prayers include almsgiving.

89. OS 11, p. 42; translation—Elsie Anne McKee, "John Calvin on the Diaconate and Liturgical Almsgiving," (Ph.D. diss, Princeton Theological Seminary, 1982) p. 50-51.

90. 3.20.33, 4.10.30, 3.25.5, 8.

91. 4.10.1, 8, 16, 27, 29, 31, 32. "...it is not our task to bind with new bonds consciences that Christ most sternly forbids to enslave," 3.4.13, 3.19.7ff. See also Bowen, who asserts that adiaphoric ceremonies, for example, are those that are neither commanded nor prohibited by scripture, are not offensive to our neighbor, and are not sterile, that is, they have some edifying or other value that enhances the dialogue we have described.

92. 4.10.30, 3.20.29, 4.3.10, 4.10.27ff. Bouwsma finds the notion of decorum as a kind of fitting accommodation rooted in the rhetorical tradition, a key theme in Calvin.

93. 2.6.1; this in response to the question of the validity of Old Testament worship patterns that were valid precisely because they did look to Christ. Christ is the furfillment of all such rites, that are accordingly no longer in use (above). Yet the same essential worship is required, only the form has changed as God's accommodation to new and different human capacities.

94. 2.16.1.

95. Christ *is* salvation, 1.13.13, 2.16.19, 3.4.25, 3.5.3.

96. 2.15.6, 3.4.4. This is fundamental to Calvin's argument against the Roman priesthood. Christ alone is a true priest, and because all who are joined to him share in his benefits, all share in that priesthood. There can be no intermediary between us and Christ, 4.19.25, 28. The other issue is, of course, the mistaken idea of the mass being a sacrifice in some way along with Christ's own, 4.18.1.

97. "...we see that whatever is of God is attributed to Christ," 1.13.24, etc. In 1.13.13 Calvin engages in an uncharacteristic bit of *lex orandi*: "But the name of Christ is invoked for salvation; therefore it follows that he is Jehovah." He also notes "...the salutations prefixed to the letters of Paul pray for the same benefits from the Son as from the Father," 1.13.13. The baptismal formula attests the same, and includes the Spirit. 1.13.16, 17.

98. 3.20.17.

99. Preface, p. 13.

100. 2.8.11.

101. 2.8.40; God's image, given in creation, is spiritual, 1.15.3, although it is expressed in obedience to the law, 2.8.51; God's image was *not* totally obliterated in the fall, 1.15.4; we are to address all people in reference to that image, 3.7.6. Still, we are not to worship the image in humankind but Godself. Calvin also argues that one purpose of the Sabbath is to ensure a day of rest for all who work "under the authority of others, that they should have some respite from toil," 2.8.28, 32. Thus even where the Decalogue has to do with our direct address of God, our human relationships are considered.

102. 2.8. 9.

103. 2.8.55.

104. 4.18.16. See also 2.8.54: "our life shall best conform to God's will and the prescription of the law when it is in every respect most fruitful for our brethren." And, "all should be contemplated in God, not in themselves....whatever the character of the man, we must yet love him because we love God," 2.8.55; our gifts are to be shared, 3.7.5, 6; indeed, we are our neighbor's debtor, 2.8.46, 3.7.7. See also 4.20.1ff, where Calvin addresses civil government in this same vein.

105. "...there is nothing in which we can benefit our brethren more than in commending them to the providential care of the best of parents..." 3.20.38. Prayer especially enables us to help even those whom we do not know are in need, for we can pray generically, 3.20.39.

106. That Calvin insists that the office of deacon is meant to be one of caring of the poor instead of engaging in Sunday morning technicalities, along with identifying almsgiving as part of worship reminds us that worship includes the lateral, external dimension, 4.3.9, 4.4.1, 4.19.32. See also McKee.

107. 4.20.15.

108. 4.15.13. Fasting, however, is *not* to be considered a form of worship, 4.12.19. Yet worship is the goal of all activities, 2.8.16, 3.7.1.

109. 3.20.13.

VI

WORSHIP AS THE ENLARGEMENT OF GOD'S GRACIOUSNESS TOWARD HUMANKIND

> *For this reason, The Lord Jesus, wishing to give an example by which the world would understand that he came to enlarge rather than to limit the Father's mercy, tenderly embraces the infants offered to him....*[1]

Core Theology

With this text Calvin seeks to justify the baptizing of the infants of Christian parents. More importantly, the text concisely states one essential theological direction in which Calvin moves, even if he does not quite go the distance and at times falls back on more limited perspectives. For Calvin, worship events uniquely express the conviction that Christ Jesus came to enlarge God's graciousness toward humankind. Dialogical, loving relationship between God and humanity is the goal of this enlargement. In this chapter, we shall see that it is precisely this dynamic perception of worship that provides significant insights and values for contemporary worship life.

Calvin remains astounded by the extent to which he has experienced the graciousness of God. This divine accommodation has been attested again and again in God's bending over backward to embrace in loving relationship what Calvin views as poor, incapacitated and sin-infested humanity. Each accommodation—the law, scripture, Jesus of Nazareth, the Spirit, the church, preaching, sacraments, human ministry—manifests one constant over time: the objective reality of God's incredible hunger for and graciousness toward humanity so that we might live in loving relationship with God and one another. But each accommodation also functions subjectively as an enlargement of God's love toward humankind, and as an experience of God's relating with us as total persons within our particular contexts. Calvin's message is clear. As was true for those before us, gracious God is here for us in our circumstances, at whatever level we are, in whatever desperate straits we are found. God so hungers to embrace us and nourish us in the relationship that makes us truly human, that God makes the divine self accessible to us so that we might truly live.

In the face of the human condition, scripture offers Christ and all Christ's benefits to us in relational encounter. This encounter becomes both the context and content of worship for Calvin. More clearly and holistically than scripture does, corporate worship expresses God's loving self-giving in the relational acts of preaching and celebrations at font and table. Yet at the same time, this divine self-giving manifests itself paradoxically in primal human behavior such as conversing, engaging with water, eating and drinking together. This results in these events taking on the character of human response, human confession, thanks and praise. In yet another turn of the paradox, prayer, our chief means of approaching God, is first given to us by God. With preaching and sacraments, prayer serves as an essential medium through which we may access the treasures of God's goodness. In other words, worship "contains," to use Calvin's own term, both God's primary, ongoing acts of love toward us in the face of our wretchedness, *and* our secondary, responsive address of God. Although God always begins these events with "I love you," from that point on God's act and our response do not happen for us so much in chronological sequence, but in dialogue, conversation, as particular moments of the ongoing relational event between God and creature. Furthermore, because life with God includes relationship with neighbor, worship is also a relational event with others of humankind. Thus we see that worship bespeaks neither one dimension, univocality, nor unidirectionality. Rather it is a multifaceted whole formed from the interweaving of God's ongoing, initiating acts of love toward us, our experiences of that love, and the relationships that result.

These two principles underwrite Calvin's entire understanding of the nature and use of worship: (1) that human being as undeniably corporeal, limited, sinful is gathered up in ongoing conversation with God by virtue of God's astonishing gifts of life-giving relationship; (2) that relationship is in fact multi-dimensional in nature because being in loving relationship with God means being in loving relationship with all of humankind.[2] Christ sums up these principles, because Christ embodies God's love from the beginning of time until the end. Therefore Christ provides the intrinsic content of worship. Worship shows forth Christ, worship offers Christ, worship leads to Christ, worship unites us with Christ. So also worship is communal because bound to Christ we are bound to one another. Finally, worship as response is affection for God expressed in a Christ-like life of prayer and obedience manifest in loving care of all of humankind.

Norms

Within that *gestalt*, of course, we find a set of norms. Corporate worship does what it does in regard to Christ because for Calvin it is largely comprised of the pure preaching of scripture as the Word of God, the right celebrating of sacraments, and authentic, heartfelt prayer. God has purposely and freely given us these events as vehicles, occurrences of gracious relationship with God and others. Each of these acts has as its fundamental purpose the offer of Christ to the individual in order to effect intimate relationship with God or to confirm and strengthen us in that relationship. We cannot replace that content in Christian worship because it constitutes the essence of Christianity. However, we must also attend to the fact that God comes *to us*, accommodates the divine self *to us*. This means that we preach gospel, celebrate sacraments and pray not only as part of the ongoing relationship between God and humanity, but precisely as moments of encounter and relationship with God *in the midst of and in conversation with the realities of those assembled*. We do not set the rest of our life aside in our meeting with God. No, in the totality of our being God engages us in love.

The *how* of these things points directly to the mysterious working of the Spirit. Nothing in worship happens without this impetus, energy, charism. The Spirit represents the ongoing accommodative character of God for us, and consequently, the "form" of worship, and the precise expression of its content remains fluid. Yet this dynamic openness always retains coherence with the Christological content, with the fundamental offer of gospel.

Use of Scripture

Calvin informs us that our use of scripture in worship is first of all bound to the comprehension that scripture is God's gift to us, that in it God provides us with knowledge of our condition and of God *pro nobis*, that through it God personally addresses us and offers Christ to us so that we might be *pro Deo*. Calvin will not let go of the idea that this reality is intrinsic to all of scripture, and therefore all of scripture is essential for authentic life with God. Of course it is on account of the dynamic interplay of Word, Spirit and person that we are able to find Christ anywhere and everywhere in scripture in the first place. Consequently Calvin lobbies for preaching the whole of scripture, most explicitly by means of his own habit of preaching *lectio continua*. Even apart from that, Calvin will hardly approve of a formalized, selective lectionary because (1) all of scripture is gift, (2) all of it is accessible through and made gospel for us by the Spirit, (3) all of it is necessary for authentic life.

True, this view of scripture makes it impossible for Calvin to recognize with Luther and more contemporary biblical scholars the extent of the interplay between the development of the church as culturally constructed and the development of the canon, to the degree an hermeneutic of suspicion becomes a minimal requirement for responsible address of scripture. Certainly Calvin's hermeneutic of going to every text in order to find Christ there can all too easily lead to a christologizing that is quite unfaithful to the text and to the peoples of the first testament. On the other hand, Calvin does recognize varying degrees of Christological value in scripture *in use*, based upon his understanding that God speaks to us according to our differing levels of Spirit-developed capacity. This implies that while in principle every pericope will certainly be of Christological import to some community somewhere, we may indeed find some texts obscure Christ *for us*, for our time and place. It further suggests a certain freedom from the compulsion to coerce such texts into the Christological mold, as well as a permission to set them aside from public use for the time being in favor of those pericopes that more readily do offer Christ here and now. Such a position would certainly be supported also by Calvin's conviction that God's accommodation to the capacities of those God addresses is paradigmatic for a preacher's use of scripture among any given congregation. Similarly, recognition of limited human capacities hints at allowing preachers a certain relief from having to preach texts they do not understand and cannot clarify for their people. At the same time, Calvin's perception of the nature of scripture as gift indispensable for life with God convinces him that we must continue as lifelong students of all of scripture, and mandates against ever putting aside texts for too long. A particular selection or pattern of readings such as the current common lectionary can never be considered definitive, then, because all of scripture is given as our Spirit-staffed school, because as we grow in faith we are enabled to perceive and comprehend

what we could not before, and because our realities everywhere vary and daily change. Such diversity requires a certain accommodation and flexibility in our public use of
scripture with regard to which texts we use when and how.
But we do well to give serious attention to Calvin's perspective that the focal point will ultimately be the relational
offer of Christ as the one who weaves us into loving relationship with God and neighbor.

It follows that every use of scripture in worship, and
not just in the act of preaching, requires preparation, serious, careful preparation. Scripture, to the degree we perceive it to be the Word of God, needs to be honored. More
important, to the degree that we assent that scripture is the
word of God *for us*, we need to bring it into intentional conversation with our realities so that we can comprehend and
embrace it, so that it can make sense of our lives. Furthermore, preaching in particular happens as a relational, dialogical event. Preachers do not only preach the Word for
themselves, they preach the Word with this particular people in this time and this place, so that this people may experience relationship with God now. Not only must the text
be understood, but also the diverse realities of the people
recognized, and the two considered in tandem. It will not
suffice today, any more than it did in Calvin's time, for a
preacher simply to repeat scripture. Recognizing that
preaching means to engage the whole people in exchange
with God via scripture is the only way to do justice to
God's gracious offer in scripture. That means that preaching must be dialogically, conversationally done. Addition-
ally, the Word preached enacts Christ as God's gracious offer of love toward humankind with all that implies. As such
it is an event of loving relationship with God and neighbor.
Consequently, the act of preaching needs to be lovingly
done. Manner of preparation, style, words, form, gestures,
tone of voice of the preacher as well as specific theological
content will all be considerations here, as will the active involvement of the gathered community. All aspects of
preaching need to take on the quality of that relationship

and model it visibly.

Calvin certainly expects active involvement of the people in their life outside the sanctuary doors, as well as in listening, singing, praying at the font and at the table. He does not see, however, that this mandates their active involvement in constructing sermons and the whole content of the worship event, in spite of his awareness of the importance of experience as a teacher. His pedagogy is still that of his age. Nevertheless, the measure of such an interactive event will always be that we preach and do that which proclaims and participates in the enlargement over time of the incredible graciousness of God toward us. The essential question will always be, "does this proclamatory event offer Christ, God *pro nobis* here and now in such a way that loving, life-giving relationship with God and others can occur?" As Calvin has already shown us, while ultimately that result depends upon the working of the Spirit, we are not permitted to sit back and let it happen. We are responsible for using all our resources to aid the achievement of this goal.

Sacrament

We see also that the very nature of sacrament, as Calvin understands it, reveals how sacraments can most authentically be celebrated. For Calvin, the Word as the offer of Christ informs and forms events at font and table. This makes it quite impossible for Calvin that these sacraments be celebrated apart from the preaching of the Word, of which they are the embodiment and necessary conclusion. Furthermore, while Calvin cannot admit that baptism and supper are essential for justification, he does insist nonetheless that we require them in order to truly experience holistically God's love and to participate fully in ongoing relationship with God and neighbor. If we accept these premises, we must go a step further than Calvin himself explicitly does and acknowledge that the Word preached apart from intentional, confirming embodiment is equally impossible. As Calvin claims, we do need every help we can get, including maximal corporate expressions and experiences of God *pro nobis*, in order to live the Christian life. Calvin will not be satisfied to let preaching alone suffice. Sacraments most vividly portray the enlargement of God's graciousness to the very bones of our corporeal being. If, indeed, the meal in particular concretely bodies forth loving, life-giving relationship with God and neighbor, then Calvin leaves little room for justifying the regular gathering of the body for worship as anything less than preaching and table fellowship. Why would we settle for anything less than such comprehensive, organic embodiment of love shared?

Objectively, God's Word can stand on its own because it is sacrament within itself. The reality with which we have to deal, however, is that we need concrete, bodying forth of gospel, bodying forth that invests *our* bodies fully in its doing. The all-too-common contemporary reliance on oral proclamation apart from the embodied experience of it exemplifies, from Calvin's viewpoint, a pride that claims we do not need God's gifts, an ungratefulness toward God's gifts, and a refusal to participate in the enlargement of God's graciousness so that our life with God and with neighbor may be enhanced and enriched.

For Calvin, as well as for much of the Christian tradition, the maximal approach includes preaching and font, preaching and table. But Calvin opens us to other possibilities, because of his high valuing of preaching, because of his understanding of sacrament as primordially God's gift that demonstrates the reality of God's love for us, indeed that "offers Christ" and empowers relationship with God and neighbor. If we take our corporeality as persons and community seriously, we can come to embody the Word in preaching.[3] We can develop a robust worship practice that will "vividly portray the enlargement of God's graciousness" and rehearse us in it. Empowered by the Spirit we may discover, in addition to font and table, other biblically funded sacramental activity in caring for the desperate or in liberating the oppressed, or in other activities coherent with the offer of Christ, with the embodiment of God's love for all. Perhaps if Calvin had access to contemporary knowledge, he would find difficulty in maintaining the definition of sacrament in biblical "command" and ""promise," and place increasing emphasis on the inherent nature of sacrament as embodiment of God's love as manifested in the entire ministry of Jesus. In any case, Calvin certainly knew and would affirm that because we are whole, fully corporate creatures in person and in community, we require whole, fully corporate experience of living in gospel relationship. Without that, we place in deadly jeopardy individual, communal, and even global human life.

Calvin affirms that sacraments act as medicine for the sick, medicine aimed at restoring us to wholeness by uniting us to Christ and thus enabling us to do and be for God and others what we could not before. Calvin further attests that the Spirit makes sacraments events of healing relationship in the first place. Moreover, Calvin insists that God is indeed astonishingly generous both to sin-victimized and sin-infested humankind, and in ways we cannot fully comprehend. In other words, Calvin recognizes that it is precisely the gift nature of sacraments, their significance as the widening of God's loving offer of relationship through Christ, that commends them to the suffering, the sick, the poor, the incapacitated, the sinful: to human persons.

Even as Calvin justifies infant baptism in this assurance of God's expanding love to humankind, so it would seem this to be the best possible justification for any baptism. If so, baptism as the gift of God's extraordinary love would be the most important consideration in determining when and how baptism is best administered. We would be less concerned about what we think or know about an individual or family, and more concerned about what we know about God's offer of love toward humankind. We would recognize as well that baptism is not so much something one can prepare for, as much as it is a freely given bequest. Although Calvin recognizes sacramental participation as public confession of faith, he also saw clearly that baptism's primary claim is God's offer of love to us *in our incapacity*, and God's capacity to encourage us to embrace that love. That suggests that administering baptism *as a result of* a baptizand's or family's profession of faith may manifest idolatry based on pride. Baptism can only be administered as a result of God's gracious offer. At the same time, to understand the *nature* of baptism as the sign of God's profound love and offer of multi-dimensional relationship does insist that the entire family of faith be conscious of the *use* of baptism and take thoughtful care in providing possibilities for nurturing that relationship over time. Opportunity for life-long baptismal catechesis, then, takes on critical importance.[4] Yet especially in a society as transient as ours, to refuse to administer the sign because the community cannot be absolutely certain about how that nurturing will take place may suggest something less than a firm trust in God's ability to fulfill God's promises and to nurture relationship in spite of any particular human situation. At the same time, communities do need to discover and implement ways of encouraging and enabling such life-long nurture for those who move on from their immediate care.

If the events of preaching, bath and meal, empowered by the Spirit, are indeed God's acts of love toward us, if they have the potential to empower faithfulness and create life-oriented relationship where there was none before, we must then ask how limited human creatures can restrict the invitation or exclude those who come. Calvin has said it clearly himself: God is to be experienced, and must be experienced, as gracious before anyone can come to recognition, affirmation and trust.[5] Can full access to God's gracious gifts then be denied? Can fallible, incapacitated human beings awash in their own unfaithfulness to God and neighbor, or caught up in suffering oppression, judge anyone else's faith or capacity for recognizing God *pro nobis*?

In fact we are not to examine others, Calvin insists.

Yet he struggled with a conundrum as he faced those who insisted on believer's baptism, as he resisted reductionist theology, as he sought to be faithful to scriptural witness, as he endeavored to honor God. In Jesus' invitation to infants Calvin can envision the enlargement of God's graciousness towards us as regards the baptism of infants.[6] With the table, we come to a different place. On the one hand Calvin understands the meal as God's loving gift of food and drink to those dying of hunger, thirst, and the sicknesses that come from lack of love. On the other hand he is compelled by the Pauline insistence on discernment of the body to limit access to the table.

We remember that Calvin claims the sacraments have no other ministry than that of the Word preached: both offer Christ. Yet Calvin does not countenance sending anyone away from preaching. Moreover, while the Word subjectively can stand alone, God has graced us with the sacraments because our corporeal selves need them as concrete confirmation of the promises of God's good will for us, God's love for us. Here is mercy embodied most fully, so that all our senses may grasp what our minds alone may stumble over. Yet it appears as if the Pauline "tree" hides the "forest" of Calvin''s larger view: his definitive and powerful recognition of the accommodating immensity of God's love meeting us where we are. Both this broader perspective, and Calvin's unarguable assertion of ongoing human inability to be consistently or even regularly discerning, wise or loving, makes a strong claim for trusting in God's good will toward us to extend quite beyond the bounds of our limited perceptions.

It is only in light of full-bodied experience of that love in the first place that we can recognize the graciousness of God *and* that we all are guilty, intentionally and unintentionally, of profaning the body.[7] All the more commendable to us, then, is Calvin's assessment of the value of a confession of sin *and* declaration of pardon as correlative with the supper. But he does not, I submit, advocate the former as punishment or castigation so much as an opportunity to recognize our need of God's gifts of life for us. For Calvin, confession serves as a chance to acknowledge and abhor the burdens that effect our faithlessness, to release our pain and grief about them, and to recognize and be filled by the extraordinary quality and quantity of the love of God *pro nobis*.

We are, in these latter days of the 20th century, growing in awareness of the systemic evil present in our world. While we may not account for it theologically in quite the same way Calvin did, we nonetheless are accountable for acknowledging both our victimization by evil and our conscious and unconscious complicity in it. This is especially true at a time when many congregations have abandoned confession and where lament finds no place.[8] In corporate worship the opportunity of each one to lay before God his or her particular dis-ease and alienation must be preserved. But even as I am not convinced by Calvin's arguments for predestination, neither am I convinced by his arguments for fencing the table. Although it exceeds Calvin's actual stance and practice in Geneva, I think his larger view of God's extraordinary, accommodating love allows us to argue for open commensality: freedom of access by all to the table, as apparently was the case in Strasbourg. We live in a world starving for the love Calvin so poignantly ascribes to God, a world in which domestic and social abuse, though often hidden, run rampant. This world is desperate for God to meet us where we are, in our need, through God-given acts of life-giving relationship such as Calvin describes the sacraments to be. All of us, children included, require lavish experience of God's love expressed concretely at table as well as at the font, because all of us need the same nourishment, the same embrace. Moreover, the Spirit who graciously works in infants in relation to baptism surely works as lovingly in them in regard to the table, as much as in the rest of us, to bring us to faith anew and with it all Christ's benefits.[9] Further, by extending a fervent and love-filled invitation to all, we participate in enlarging God's graciousness by attesting to God's claim of the value of human life through the endless accommodation of love that forgives, embraces, renews and supports even the worst and most incapacitated of our kind. Our practice at the table, like our practice in preaching, needs to model—make visible—what it bespeaks.

This does not imply that events of preaching, font, table are effective *ex opere operato*. Contra the doctrine of predestination both Calvin and the concept of *ex opere operato* espouse, few if any serious theologians today would dispute that human persons do have the freedom and the responsibility actively to receive that offer and embrace it or to reject it. Yet neither is Calvin misdirected by his anxiety that the sacraments might be profaned or in his insistence upon decorum in celebrations of the sacraments. Any sacrament celebrated willy-nilly, impudently, punitively or otherwise unlovingly hardly bespeaks the superabundant, prevenient graciousness of God and loving relationship in Christ. Any sacrament celebrated without recognition of our call to *live* eucharistically misses the whole point. If the signs, if the events, are, as Calvin rightly insists, to be coherent with what they signify, then all embodiments of gospel must occur in such a way that they truly express Christ, God-*pro-nobis*, along with love for and unity with God and the other.

In preaching, at table or font, God, through God's own act of self giving here and now, makes the graciousness of God *pro nobis* and beyond our comprehension available. If these activities are to attest truly to God's awesome generosity toward us, to the lavishness of God's care of us, even though the signs are deemed tokens, neither can minimalism in use be sustained. Calvin's preaching breadth, depth and frequency surely exemplify the maximal expression of divine generosity. His concern for this with regard to font and table focuses on his recognition that because the signs attest something beyond themselves they therefore must cohere with what they represent. Although Calvin admits disinterest in the mode of baptism,[10] he notes that the word *baptizo* suggests immersion. It would seem that if baptism proclaims that God really cleanses, revives, and unites us to Christ, then baptismal events will include water in sufficient quantities to manifest unmistakably what baptism says. So also the whole assembly encircling the baptismal waters will probably make a more compelling claim of our corporateness than the all too frequent pastor-font-immediate family-congregation arrangement so typical in contemporary congregations. Similarly, if the supper is an essential or even extraordinary expression of God's feeding and nourishing us in faith, then we would do well to do as Calvin wished, and celebrate it as regularly and in as table-surrounding a way as Sunday dinner. Moreover, and contrary to much contemporary practice, we will want to see that the bread and fruit of the vine are substantial enough to assure us that our deepest hungers and thirsts are fully satisfied in God and not merely tantalized. How else can the table attest viably to the richness of the banquet to which we are invited?

Furthermore, if by these actions we relate not only with God but with neighbor in intimate, personal address, then neither a single-file approach to the table nor an isolation-maintaining, no-contact passing of plates and glasses to unrecognized neighbors in the pew will suffice. In the offer of Christ and in uniting us with Christ, Calvin tells us, God meets us face to face, calls us by name, gathers us into the divine arms. So also sacraments beckon God's people to meet each other face to face, to call one another by name, authentically and graciously to offer to and receive from each other the gifts of God and to exercise accountability toward one another. Even in churches filled with "immovable" pews, congregations often manage quite dynamic exchanges of greetings of peace. Could not bread and fruit of the vine similarly be shared? As well, many congregations participate weekly in the "sacrament of the coffee hour" outside the sanctuary. Perhaps the entire worship event could process into communal space for real table-sharing. God gives us imagination and creativity, and even while keeping in mind Calvin's disapproval of creating new

ceremonies, God surely invites us to put our gifts to work
in the service of faithful, empowering worship.

Above all, because sacraments enact love, they can
therefore only be celebrated lovingly and with all the care
for, sensitivity and responsibility to others that love implies. How else shall we know that God is truly for each of
us, individually, personally, intimately? How else shall we
know that in Christ we all belong to one another? How else
shall we know how to body this Spirit forth in the world?
Ultimately, this is where our true eucharist, our true honoring of God lies: in loving care for the world.

Worship as Pedagogy

We come then to the indisputable fact that worship
teaches. Calvin is convinced of the power of the mind, the
value of the intellect, the worth of life-long education. But
he is not interested in knowledge for its own sake, nor for
the sake of human accomplishment. Rather, the purpose of
knowledge is to enable and enhance life with God and all
humanity. Calvin certainly recognizes the fact that all experience teaches. It follows, then, that worship has an educa-
tive function both by virtue of its content and also by virtue
of its form and process. Humankind learns not only from
ideas and concepts, but also from the way they are presented. Loving words are not very believable if they are said
unlovingly, if they exclude or neglect. The idea of the lavishness of God's gifts for us is not very convincing if the
signs are presented in an ungenerous or restricted manner.
Moreover, we must know about God-for-us to live in authentic relationship with God. But we cannot know about
God-for-us without the experience of God-for-us. Here,
too, there can be no easy separation. Still, Calvin clearly
distinguishes between the didacticism of the classroom and
the pedagogical effect of the worship event. We might say
that for Calvin the primary function of teaching in the
classroom is to provide knowledge about ourselves and
God so as to enhance our relationship with God. On the

other hand, the primary function of worship is to enable the experience of relationship that has the effect of enhancing knowledge of God and humankind. Such knowledge is not a matter of data, but of self-consciousness and conscious orientation toward God and other.

Calvin would never be willing to let worship teach by happenstance. Because worship does teach, we need to be intentional about that. We need to prepare for worship in light of its pedagogical effect so that what worship teaches is the truth of our experience of relationship with God in so far as we can express that truth. Consequently, a significant task of preaching is to clarify and explain scripture so that relationship can more readily occur. One can apply the same conviction to prayer texts and all other worship content and actions. While their true function is to be events of conversation and relationship, what is said and done informs the understanding of the experience and implications of that relationship. Therefore all public worship deserves careful, thoughtful preparation in advance, with a view to the full significance of word, movement, continuity. Such a practice does not preclude spontaneity or improvisation or commend the use of set texts. We engage, after all, in conversation, not recitation or performance. Nor does such preparation for worship diminish the role of the Spirit. There will be no teaching, no illumination, no conversation, no relationship without the involvement of the Spirit. Still, the fact remains that everything that occurs in worship does teach something. Therefore, part of our responsibility of obedience in honor of God and concern for others is to see that what is expressed is faithful to our experience of and intent of living with God and neighbor. We may want to examine for example, just how effectively our worship presents the full participation of the wholeness of God, Parent, Mediator, Spirit. As well, we may want to consider if our worship life in the church truly rehearses us for living lovingly with our global neighbors.

Affections of the Heart

It will not suffice to do things correctly, to teach rightly. Worship remains for Calvin a matter of the God-given affections of the heart: God's affection for humankind, and ours for God and all humanity. We have already indicated that authentic worship manifests God's affections toward us. So also worship as our response must be faithful to and embodying of our affections toward God and others. Trust, integrity, gratitude, love—these are paramount for Calvin. But if God embraces us as whole beings in our reality, then surely our whole emotional life rests with God. Integrity demands that when we engage in worship privately or corporately, all our feelings rightly belong to our conversation with God. If we are full of ingratitude, what could be more impious than to refuse to admit it, to pretend to be thankful? If we are full of hate, what could be more profane than to lie about it, to refuse to engage in conversation that acknowledges it? So again Calvin commends confession to us, and implicitly, not only songs of joy, thanks and praise, but in accord with the psalter, expressions of lament, fear, pain and confusion. Similarly, if Easter has occurred for us today but the calendar tells us it is Good Friday, would God have us stifle our joy any more than pretend to mourn? Quite the contrary. If we agree with Calvin that worship arises in the heart, if we affirm that our whole being rests with God, and if we attest to the relational nature of worship, we will also recognize that whatever the tenor of worship of a given day, space needs to be provided for the expression of alternate feelings and affections. If the body at large sings and dances with joy, accommodation must be made for those immobilized with grief and dumb with pain. Alternately, in the face of death, the experience of life needs room for celebration. Our realities *are* our realities, and our affections and emotions in their diversity and fullness belong to our wholeness. If we affirm with Calvin that God embraces us as whole persons, we are compelled to recognize that the full range of human emotions, affections

and actions belong part and parcel to our worship as authentic, honest relationship with God and neighbor. Contemporary worship design will be less than faithful to the
full claim of gospel if it does not intentionally embrace all
that we are as human beings.

Worship as Life in the World

Worship for Calvin begins with God addressing us,
embracing us via word, table, hymn, prayer, but it only begins there. Calvin will not allow us to confine worship to
Sunday morning in the pews, any more than he will permit
us to attempt to localize Christ in sacramental elements, the
Spirit in an *epiclesis*, or God in scripture. God's self-giving
is available to us fundamentally and is most intensely focused and therefore able to be grasped by us when the community gathers for the event of gospel in word and act. But
this loving, self-giving God also makes the divine self accessible to us in our private prayer, scripture reading, and in
tender loving care given to us by others. In mirror image,
the gathered community serves as the initial locus of our responsive address of God. However, through Calvin's emphasis on God's acts toward us when the community gathers, Calvin lets us know that we most fully and completely
engage in worship as response to God, *outside the* gathered
community, in a eucharistic life. God's graciousness expressed in the gifts comprising a worship gathering, and our
relational interaction around them limn our life in the
world. Worship occasions "teach" by forming us in atti-
tudes, dispositions and intentions through primary experience. We will most authentically and fully make known in
the world our affections of the heart by the way we conduct
ourselves in daily living toward others. Through the valuing of the lives of others no matter how marginal or deca-
dent they seem to us, we will live out our thanksgiving for
the gift of life with God. We will further extend the enlargement of God's graciousness to us by our graciousness
toward others, regardless of human definitions of those others' worth.

We cannot, as Calvin clearly sees, live in authentic, loving relationship with God or worship God faithfully if we do not endeavor mightily to live in loving relationship with humankind and individual persons. Our worship in the sanctuary and our worship in the world, though distinguishable, are inseparable, for worship is the sum of Christian life. Yes, Calvin delineates an undeniable tension between spirit and flesh. The fact that we have to do with a Spirit-natured ultimacy is beyond question for him. Yet we see here as well his claim of the reality of the interplay between body and spirit, spiritual divinity and corporeal humanity, as well as God-relatedness and other-relatedness. In fact, for Calvin the corporeality of the entirety of public worship, powerfully expresses the reality of the wholeness of life. Ultimately this leads to an affirmation of the wholeness of personhood as integration of spirit and body. Moreover, the entirety of corporate worship inclusive of God's gifts and our response functions as a microcosm of the whole life in God bodied forth in the full range of daily activity.

An Ecosystem Beginning with God's Act

We treat here a theological whole, an ecosystem in which every element is visible, perhaps, but clearly not separable from the rest. In the first place, no worship happens without the full participation of God our gracious Parent, Christ our Loving Mediator, the Spirit as the Empowerer, and faithful Christians. We cannot really think of worship so much as a chronological sequence of God's acts and ours, as distinct within the gathered community from outside it, but only as a multi-dimensional interrelationship in which every element and aspect converses with and breathes life into every other. While affections, obedience, prayer, public worship with its many embodiments, private worship, honoring God and caring for others are all distinguishable elements of worship, they cannot be separated from each other. All these elements are fully interwoven within the whole of worship corporate and individual. Nev-

ertheless, Calvin would not have us lose sight of the primacy of God's gifts for us in corporate worship, nor the fact
that it is relationship with God that both enables and requires our loving relationship with our own kind. In practi-
cal terms, such a recognition has significance in contemporary worship life particularly in the arranging and naming
of worship elements so that we do not confuse gift with response nor mistake the worship of the public assembly as
the end rather than the beginning of our life with God and
all humankind. So, we can no longer speak of preaching
and sacrament, but perhaps of enactments of gospel. We
can no longer speak of worship as a discrete event or pattern of events, but only of worship events, microcosms of
the macrocosm of worshipful, eucharistic life.

Unresolved Tensions

There can be no denying that tensions remain. Calvin's *Institutes* teem with polemical charges between Calvin and Rome, Calvin and the Anabaptists, Calvin and his
fellow reformers, Calvin and the town fathers, and even
Calvin and Calvin[11] regarding the nature and use of worship. Some of the more obvious indicators include: 1) Calvin's inconsistent use of scripture, 2) the contradiction between a God so gracious as to accommodate to our every
need yet so ungracious (though Calvin did not think it so)
as to use preaching to harden the hearts of some and the
supper to poison some, 3) the lack of clarity about the nature of baptism as gift and the demand for faith as a pre-
requisite, 4) the confusion over the membership in the body
brought about by baptism and that attested in the supper, 5)
the disparity between flesh versus spirit with the recognition of human as both and as such, embraced by God. Yet
even here Calvin offers us a useful guide: these tensions result for us from the reality of human life. We can never be
sure we have the issues quite straight, the concepts quite
clear, the practice quite perfect. As adamant as Calvin is
about his views, as much as he values some of those who
have gone before him, he recognizes too well the fallibility

of human nature, although perhaps not well enough the drive to develop and grow. In any case, Calvin revises the *Institutes* again and again, he makes recourse repeatedly to scripture, to the traditions of the church, to reason, to experience. Calvin weighs and challenges assumptions, asks rhetorical questions (that are rarely if ever merely rhetorical questions). Calvin offers the Form of Church Prayers as a model, mutable, fluid, optional.

Towards the Future

As much as Calvin was horrified at the rending of the church, nevertheless we can see, if he could not, the value of controversy as leading us to new considerations and growth in faithfulness. Far from recommending a polemical spirit such as that of the sixteenth century reformation in Europe, nevertheless we can affirm and encourage a healthy tension that challenges us to think again about interpretations of scriptural texts, hermeneutical approaches, liturgical constructs, values, patterns. In the actuality of a partially realized eschatology that is ours as much as it was Calvin's, we do well to restrain from the establishing of definitive norms and criteria for worship that extend beyond Calvin's fundamental values. These include the basic relational, accommodating, extraordinarily loving claim of gospel manifest in preaching, sacraments, prayer, and eucharistic life informed by the affections of the heart and aimed toward the enlargement of God's graciousness toward humankind. In recognition of our fluid and diverse contexts, we do well to restrain from making commitments to a particular selection of texts or a pattern of worship as valid for all times and all places. If nothing else, in evidencing the love of God toward often unlovable humanity, gospel itself shows its tendency to stand in opposition to human claims and to contradict human expectations and requirements. Furthermore, if God is the extraordinarily gracious God Calvin claimed, and if God truly accommodates the divine self to different realities, if the Spirit is always at work in the world, then diversity is inherent in the

divine nature. We can never assume that any particular
means of embodying gospel and enlarging God's graciousness toward humankind that applies today will do so tomor-
row.

Thus we conclude that for Calvin and for us, the
pristinam normam of worship is not, in fact, forms or texts
or any set of patterns, but a theological whole created by its
content. Furthermore, it is not content in detail that is essential—this prayer, that sequence of components, "the institution narrative"—but content writ large. The content is
at the first level Christ as the accommodating enlargement
of God's astounding graciousness toward us; Christ as the
one who fulfills the promises of God toward us and who
brings us to and sustains us in life-giving relationship with
God and others. At the second level, the content is all the
embodiments of gospel in worship event and in eucharistic
life, rooted in the affections of the heart, energized by the
Spirit, enacted lovingly and accommodatingly so that
God's gifts toward us are truly evident and loving relationship with God and all humankind is truly possible.

Because gospel means living relationship in the
context of diverse realities, worship content can only be expressed in diversity, in changing patterns and postures that
embrace the engagement of God with us amidst our particular realities. The details of expression of God *pro nobis* and
of humankind *pro Deo* will always be shaped first by the
content of accommodating love and then by the realities of
the people involved here and now. It will never suffice to
know what Christians thought about or how they practiced
baptism or supper or preaching or prayer in the first or the
fourth or the sixteenth centuries or even in the last generation or at the church down the block. Nor will it suffice to
claim freedom from traditional patterns and texts as justification for doing what we please. It will only suffice to
know whether Christ is preached, offered now, if loving
God is encountered here, if God's graciousness toward humankind is enlarged, if relationship with God and the
whole family of God in the world is somehow enabled and

sustained in this time and place. Because we are who we are—shaped by our own human being, by time, culture, geography, and endlessly vulnerable to sin—the questions must always be asked anew.

NOTES

1. 4.16.7.

2. Gerrish sums these up neatly with the title of his book, *Grace and Gratitude.*

3. See my *A Kinesthetic Homiletic: Embodying Gospel in Preaching.* Minneapolis: Fortress Press. 1993.

4. Luther intended his catechism to provide life-long learning and support for every member of the church.

5. 1.2.1.

6. Children do belong to the covenant and therefore should not be forbidden the sign. More importantly, they are children of Adam and their only recourse to life is Christ. And since Christ himself beckons them, how then shall they be denied? 4.16.17.

7. As Gerrish puts it, "The pious mind...is a pious mind only because it has tasted the father's goodness." *Grace and Gratitude,* p. 69.

8. See Don E. Saliers, *Worship Come to Its Senses,* Abingdon Press, 1996, and Ward, Richard Finley, "Mourning at Eastertide: Revisiting a Broken Liturgy," *Worship,* Vol. 71, #2 (March, 1997) for thoughtful addresses of the role of lament in worship.

9. Gerrish claims rightly, I think, that Calvin found "that it is not God's judicial person but God's fatherly person that determines the life of true piety." Elsewhere he notes "Not the divine despot but the Parent -God, who is goodness itself, was the object of Calvin's piety and therefore the main theme of his doctrine of God." *Grace and Gratitude,* p. 60; p. 41. This simply affirms what we have said all along.

10. 4.15.19.

11. See Bouwsma for a thorough articulation of intra-Calvin tension.

BIBLIOGRAPHY

Primary Sources

Calvin, John. *Opera Selecta*, 5 Vol., ed. Petrus Barth, *et al*; and *Ioannis Calvini Opera quae supersunt omnia*, in the *Corpus Reformatorum*, vol. 29-87.

.... *A Selection of the Most Celebrated Sermons*, James A. Bill, tr., ed. Philadelphia: 1847.

.... "Catechismus Ecclesiae Genevensis," OS, Vol. ll. "The Catechism of the Church of Geneva, that is, a Plan for Instructing Children in the Doctrine of Christ," in *Calvin: Theological Treatises*, J.K.S. Reid, ed., The Library of Christian Classics: Ichthus Edition, Philadelphia: The Westminster Press, 1954.

.... "The Clear Explanation of Sound Doctrine Concerning the True Partaking of the Flesh and Blood of Christ in the Holy Supper (to dissipate the mists of Tileman Heshusius)," (1561) in *Calvin: Theological Treatises*, J.K.S. Reid, ed. Library of Christian Classics: Ichthus Edition Philadelphia: The Westminster Press (CR9, p. 41ff).

.... *Commentaries*. Joseph Haroutunian, ed. Philadelphia: The Westminster Press, 1958. (Library of Christian Classics, Ichthus Edition).

.... *Commentary on the Epistles of Paul the Apostle to the Corinthians*, Vol. 1. Tr. John J. Pringle. Grand Rapids: Wm. B. Eerdmans Publishing Company, 1948.

.... *Commentary on A Harmony of the Evangelists, Mt. Mk., and Lk.*, Vol 3. Tr. Wm. Pringle. Grand Rapids: Wm. B. Eerdmans Publishing Co, 1949.

.... *Commentaries on the Twelve Minor Prophets*, Vol. 3. Tr. John Owen. Grand Rapids: Wm. B. Eerdmans Publishing Company, 1950

.... "The Deity of Jesus Christ," in *The Deity of Christ and Other Sermons*. Tr. Leroy Nixon. Grand Rapids: Wm. B. Eerdmans Publishing Company, 1950. (*Corpus Reformatorum, Calvini Opera*, Vol. 47).

.... "Epistle to Simon Grynaeus on the Commentary on Romans," *Calvin: Commentaries*. Joseph Haroutunian, ed. Philadelphia: The Westminster Press, 1958. (Library of Christian Classics, Ichthus Edition).

.... *Epistre au Lecteur, La Form Des Prières et Chantz Eccle-siastiques,* OS Vol. II. Tr. F. L. Battles, "John Calvin: The Form of Prayers and Songs of the Church, 1542—Letter to the Reader." *Calvin Theological Journal,* Vol. 15, No. 2 (November, 1980).

.... "Essay on the Lord's Supper, the Form of Prayers," tr. B. W. Farley, in *Calvin Studies II.* (Presented at a colloquium on Calvin Studies, at Davidson College Presbyterian Church and Davidson College, Davidson, North Carolina) 1984.

.... "The Gospel According to St. John 1-X," Tr. T.H.L. Parker. In *Calvin's Commentaries,* London: Oliver and Boyd, 1959.

.... *Institutes of the Christian Religion.* John T. McNeill, ed; F. L. Battles, Tr. (from the 1559 Latin Text edited by Barth and Niesel, [*Ioannis Calvini Opera Selecta* Vol. 3, 4, 5. Munich: Chr. Kaiser, 1926-1952] including collations from earlier editions of that text and versions of the *Institutes*). The Library of Christian Classics, Vol. XX and XI, Philadelphia: The Westminster Press, 1960.

.... *La Form Des Prières et Chantz Ecclesiastiques, Ioannis Calvini Opera Selecta,* 5 Vols. Petrus Barth, Guilelmus Niesel, and Dora Scheuner, eds. Monachii: Chr. Kaiser, 1926-1952; Vol. ll, p. 11ff. Bard Thompson, ed., "The Form of Church Prayers and Hymns with the Manner of Administering the Sacraments and Consecrating Marriage According to the Custom of the Ancient Church," in *Liturgies of the Western Church,* NY: World Publishing Company, 1960.

.... "Preface to Olivetan's New Testament," *Calvin: Commentaries.* Joseph Haroutunian, ed. Philadelphia: The Westminster Press, 1958. (Library of Christian Classics, lchthus Edition).

.... *Sermons on Isaiah's Prophecy of the Death and Passion of Christ,* T.H.L. Parker, Tr. ed. London: James Clarke & Co. Ltd. 1956.

Secondary Sources

Anderson, Luke. "The *Imago Dei* Theme in John Calvin and Bernard of Clairvaux" in *Calvinus Sacrae Scripturae Professor: Calvin as Confessor of Holy Scripture.* Wilhelm H. Neuser, ed. Grand Rapids: Wm. B. Eerdmans Publishing Company, 1994.

Balke, W., "The Word of God and Experientia according to Calvin," in *Calvinus Ecclesiae Doctor. Die Referate des Congrès International de Recherches Calviniennes.* W.H. Neuser, ed. Uitgeversmaatschappij: J.H. Kok B.V., 1978.

Baptism, Eucharist and Ministry. Faith and Order Paper No. 111, World Council of Churches, Geneva, 1982.

Battles, Ford Lewis. *Calculus Fidei: Some Ruminations on the Structure of the Theology of John Calvin,* Grand Rapids: Calvin Theological Seminary, 1978. The latter is found also in *Calvinus Ecclesiae Doctor.*

.... "God Was Accommodating Himself to Human Capacity," *Readings in Calvin's Theology,* Donald K. McKim, ed. Grand Rapids: Baker Book House. 1984. Reprinted from *Interpretation,* Vol. 31 (January, 1977).

Bouwsma, William J. *John Calvin: A Sixteenth-Century Portrait.* NY: Oxford U. Press, 1988.

Bowen, David Anderson. *John Calvin's Ecclesiological Adiaphorism: Distinguishing the "Indifferent," the "Essential," and the "Important" in His Thought and Practice.* Ann Arbor: University Microfilms International, 1985.

Brunner, Peter. *Worship in the Name of Jesus.* St. Louis: Concordia Publishing House, 1968. Tr. M.H. Bertram: Zur Lehre vom Gottesdienst der im Namen Jesu versammelten Gemeinde in *Leiturgia, Handbook des evangelischen Gottesdienstes,* Vol. 1. Kassel: Johannes Stauda Verlag, 1954. Karl Ferdinand Müller and Walter Blankenburg, eds.

Burkhart, John E. *Worship: A Searching Examination of the Liturgical Experience.* Philadelphia: Westminster Press, 1982.

Butin, Philip Walker. *Calvin, The Trinity, and the Divine-Human Relationship.* Ph.D. Diss. Duke University. Ann Arbor: UMI Dissertation Services, 1991.

Dempsey Douglass, Jane, "The Image of God in Humanity: A Comparison of Calvin's Teaching in 1536 and 1559." *Papers from the 1986 International Calvin Symposium.* E.J. Furcha, ed. FRS/ARC 1987.

Eire, Carlos M.N. "Calvin's Attack on Idolatry," in *John Calvin and the Church: A Prism of Reform.* Timothy George, ed. Louisville: W/JKP, 1990.

Forstman, H. Jackson. *Word and Spirit: Calvin's Doctrine of Biblical Authority.* Stanford: Stanford University Press, 1962.

Gamble, Richard C., ed. *Calvin's Ecclesiology: Sacraments end Deacons. In Articles on Calvin and Calvinism,* Vol. 10. NY: Garland Publishing, Inc. 1992.

Gerrish, B.A. *Grace and Gratitude: The Eucharistic Theology of John Calvin.* Minneapolis: Fortress, 1993.

Gerrish, B.A. cont'd.

............"John Calvin and the Reformed Doctrine of the Lord's Supper." *McCormick Quarterly* Vol 22, 1969. (Also reprinted as "Gospel and Eucharist: John Calvin on the Lord's Supper") in Gerrish, B. A. *The Old Protestantism and the New*, Chicago: The University of Chicago Press, 1982.

.... "The Mirror of God's Goodness: A Key Metaphor in Calvin's View of Man," in *Readings in Calvin's Theology*, Donald K. McKim, ed. Grand Rapids: Baker Book House, 1984. (Reprinted from *The Old Protestantism and the New*, Chicago: University of Chicago, 1982. Originally published in *Concordia Theological Quarterly*, 45 (July, 1981).

.... "The Word of God and the Words of Scripture: Luther and Calvin on Biblical Authority," in *The Old Protestantism and the New*, Chicago: University of Chicago Press, 1982.

Gerstner, John H. "Calvin's Two-Voice Theory of Preaching," in *Articles on Calvin and Calvinism*, Vol. 10: *Ecclesiology: Sacraments end Deacons*. Richard C. Gamble, ed. NY: Garland Publishing, Inc. 1992.

Grout, Jay. *A History of Western Music*. NY: W.W. Norton & Company, Inc. 1960.

Hageman, Howard G. *Pulpit and Table: Some Chapters in the History of Worship in the Reformed Churches*. Richmond: John Knox Press, 1962.

Holifield, E. Brooks. "John Calvin," in *The Covenant Sealed: The Development of Puritan Sacramental Theology in Old and New England, 1570-1720*. New Haven: Yale University Press, 1974.

Kraus, Hans-Joachim. "Calvin's Exegetical Principles," *Interpretation* Vol. 31 (1977). Tr. Keith Crim.

Krusche, Werner. *Das Wirken des Heiligen Geistes nach Calvin*. Göttingen: Vandenhoeck and Ruprecht, 1957.

Lehman, Paul. "The Reformers' Use of the Bible," *Theology Today*, Vol. 3 (1946-7).

Leith, John H. "Calvin's Doctrine of the Proclamation of the Word and Its Significance for Today in the Light of Recent Research," in *Calvin Studies II* (Presented at a Colloquium on Calvin Studies at Davidson College Presbyterian Church and Davidson College, Davidson, North Carolina). John H. Leith, ed. 1984.

Maxwell, William D. "Calvin's French Rites at Strasbourg and Geneva," in *An Outline of Christian Worship: Its Development and Forms*. London: Oxford University Press, 1936, 1939.

McDonnell, Kilian. O.S.B. "Calvin's Eucharistic Doctrine," in *Reformed Liturgies,* Vol. 5, #2, Fall, 1986.

.... "Calvin's Conception of the Liturgy and the Future of the Roman Catholic Liturgy," *Reformed Liturgies,* Vol. 5, #2, Fall 1986 (Reprinted by permission of *Concilium,* Revue Internationale de Théologie, Arksteestraat 3-5, Nijmegen (Holland); Feb. 1969.

McKee, Elsie Anne. "John Calvin's Teaching on the Lord's Prayer." *The Princeton Seminary Bulletin.* Supplement; #2, 1992.

McKim, Donald K. "Calvin's View of Scripture," in *Readings in Calvin's Theology,* Grand Rapids: Baker Book House, 1984.

.... "John Calvin: A Theologian for an Age of Limits," in *Readings in Calvin's Theology,* Grand Rapids: Baker Book House, 1984.

McNeill, John T. "The Significance of the Word of God for Calvin," *Church History,* Vol. 28 (1959).

Moltman, Jürgen. *The Crucified God.* NY: Harper and Row, Publishers, 1974. (*Der gekreuzigte Gott.* Tr. R. A. Wilson and John Bowden. Munich: Christian Kaiser Verlag. 1973).

Muller, Richard A. "The Foundation of Calvin's Theology: Scripture as Revealing God's Word." *Duke Divinity School Review,* Vol. 44 (Winter, 1979).

Neuser, Wilhelm H., "Calvins Verständnis der Heiligen Schrift." *Calvinus Sacrae Scripturae Professor: Calvin as Confessor of Holy Scripture.* Wilhelm H. Neuser, ed. Die Referate des Congrès International des Recherches Calviniennes Vom 20. bis 23. August, 1990. Grand Rapids: William B. Eerdmans Publishing Company, 1994.

Nichols, James H. "The Intent of the Calvinistic Liturgy," in *The Heritage of John Calvin,* John H. Bratt, ed. Grand Rapids: Wm. B. Eerdmans Publishing Company. 1973.

Niesel, Wilhelm. "The Sacraments," in *Readings in Calvin's Theology,* Grand Rapids: Baker Book House, 1984.

Old, Hughes Oliphant. *Leading in Prayer: A Workbook for Worship.* Grand Rapids: Wm. B. Eerdmans Publishing Co., 1995.

.... *The Patristic Roots of Reformed Worship.* Zürich: Theologischer Verlag, 1970, 1975.

.... *The Shaping of the Reformed Baptismal Rite in the Sixteenth Century.* Grand Rapids: Wm. B. Eerdmans Publishing Company, 1992.

Old, Hughes Oliphant, Cont.
.... *Themes & Variations for a Christian Doxology: Some Thoughts on the Theology of Worship.* Grand Rapids: Wm. B. Eerdmans Publishing Company, 1992.
.... *Worship that is Reformed According to Scripture.* Atlanta: John Knox Press, *Guides to the Reformed Tradition,* John H. Leith & John W. Kuykendall, eds. 1984.
Osmer, Richard Robert. *A Teachable Spirit: Recovering the Teaching Office in the Church.* Louisville: WJK, 1990.

Parker, T.H.L. *John Calvin: A Biography.* Philadelphia: Westminster Press, 1975.
.... *Calvin's Preaching.* Louisville: Westminster/John Knox Press for T&T Clark, 1992.
.... *The Oracles of God: An introduction to the Preaching of John Calvin.* London: Lutterworth Press, 1975.
Pasztor, Janos. "Calvin and the Renewal of the Worship of the Church." *Reformed World.* Vol. 2 (1988).
Peter, Rodolph. "Calvin and Liturgy, According to the *Institutes,*" *John Calvin's Institutes His Opus Magnum.* Proceedings of the Second South African Congress for Calvin Research, July 31-August 3, 1984. Potchefstroom: Potchefstroom University for Christian Higher Education, 1986.
.... "Rhétorique Et Prédication Selon Calvin," *Revue D'Histoire et de Philosophie Religieuses* #2, Vol. 55 (1975).

Raitt, Jill. "Three Inter-related Principles in Calvin's Unique Doctrine of Infant Baptism," *Sixteenth Century Journal,* Vol. Xl, #1 (1980).
Reid, J.K.S. "Calvin on the Authority of Holy Scripture." *The Authority of Scripture: A Study of the Reformation and Post-Reformation Understanding of the Bible.* NY: Harper & Brothers, 1957.
.... "Gospel and Eucharist," in *Gospel and Sacrament.* Günther Gassmann and Vilmos Vajta, eds. *Oecumenica.* Minneapolis: Augsburg Publishing House, 1970.
Riggs, John W. "The Development of Calvin's Baptismal Theology, 1536-1560," (Ph.D. Diss., University of Notre Dame, 1986) .
.... "Emerging Ecclesiology in Calvin's Baptismal Thought, 1536-1543," *Church History,* Vol. 64, #1 (March 1995).
Rogers, Jack B. and Donald K. McKim. *The Authority and Interpretation of the Bible: An Historical Approach.* San Francisco: Harper & Row, Publishers, 1979.

Saliers, Don E. *Worship Come to Its Senses*. Nashville: Abingdon Press, 1996.
Shepherd, Victor A. *The Nature and Function of Faith in John Calvin*. Macon, Ga: Mercer U. Press, 1983.
Spinks, Bryan D. "Calvin's Baptismal Theology and the Making of the Strasbourg and Genevan Baptismal Liturgies 1540 and 1542," *Scottish Journal of Theology*, Vol. 48, #1 (1995).
Stauffer, Richard. "L'Homilétique de Calvin," in *Interprètes de la Bible: Études sur les Réformateurs du XVIᵉ Siècle*. Paris: Éditions Beuchesne, 1980.

Thomas, Thomas Forsyth. *The Hermeneutics of John Calvin*. Edinburgh: Scottish Academic Press, 1988.
Thompson, Bard, ed. *Liturgies of the Western Church*, NY: World Publishing Company, 1960.
Tylenda, Joseph N. "Calvin and Christ's Presence in the Supper—True or Real," in *Articles on Calvin and Calvinism, Vol. 10: Ecclesiology: Sacraments and Deacons*. Richard C. Gamble, ed. NY: Garland Publishing, Inc., 1992.
.... "Calvin's Understanding of the Communication of Properties," *Westminster Theological Journal*, Vol. 38 (1975-76).

van der Walt, A.G.P. "Calvin on Preaching," *John Calvin's Institutes His Opus Magnum*. Potchefstroom: Potchefstroom University for Christian Higher Education. 1986.
Velthuysen, G.C. "Ministries of the Spirit: Calvin on the Sacraments." *John Calvin's Institutes His Opus Magnum*. Potchefstroom: Potchefstroom University for Christian Higher Education. 1986.

Wainwright, Geoffrey. *Doxology: The Praise of God in Worship, Doctrine and Life: A Systematic Theology*. NY: Oxford University Press, 1980.
Walker, G.S.M. "Calvin and the Church," in McKim, Donald K. "Calvin's View of Scripture," *Readings in Calvin's Theology*, Donald K. McKim, ed. Grand Rapids: Baker Book House. 1984.
.... "The Lord's Supper in the Theology and Practice of Calvin," in *John Calvin*, G.E. Duffield, ed. Grand Rapids: Wm. B. Eerdmans Publishing Co. 1966.
Wallace, Ronald S. *Calvin's Doctrine of The Word and Sacrament*. Tyler, TX: Geneva Divinity School Press, 1982. (Originally published in 1953 by Oliver and Boyd, Ltd., Edinburgh).

Wallace, Ronald S., Cont.

.... "The Preached Word as the Word of God," in McKim, Donald K. "Calvin's View of Scripture," *Readings in Calvin's Theology*, Donald K. McKim, ed. Grand Rapids: Baker Book House, 1984.

Ward, Richard Finley. "Mourning at Eastertide: Revisiting a Broken Liturgy." *Worship*, Vol. 71, #2 (March 1997).

White, James F. *Sacraments as God's Self Giving*. Nashville: Abingdon, 1983.

Willis, D. "Calvin's Use of Substantia," in *Calvinus Ecclesiae Genevensis Custos*, Wilhelm H. Neuser, ed. Frankfurt am Main: Verlag Peter Lang, 1982.

INDEX

Accommodates, 16-18, 71, 85, 88, 106, 111, 132, 137, 154, 171

Accommodation, 16, 18-20, 22-24, 27, 28, 38, 39, 42, 45, 48, 61, 66, 91, 98, 104, 109, 126, 129-131, 139, 151, 152, 155, 156, 163, 167

Adoption, 24, 40

Affections, 93, 122, 124, 142, 167-169, 171, 172

Art, 127

Arts, 18, 72, 136

Assembly, 99, 107, 133, 134, 137, 142, 144, 164, 170

Augustine, 5, 18, 42, 65, 67, 69, 70, 72, 93, 102, 123

Baptism, ix, 3, 36, 37, 56, 76, 88, 89, 90, 91, 93, 95, 96, 99-101, 103-105, 107-109, 111, 120, 136, 137, 157, 159-164, 170, 172

Bath, 36, 37, 98, 101, 103, 105, 134, 160

Benefits, ix, 39-41, 60, 85, 88, 90, 93, 95, 101, 104, 131, 132, 136, 138-140, 152, 162

Body, 5, 6, 16, 54, 55, 67, 68, 87, 89, 91, 96-98, 100-103, 105-109, 111, 127, 142, 144, 158, 161, 165, 167, 169, 170

Bullinger, 98

Ceremonies, 88-92, 99, 102, 110, 120, 136-139, 165

Christ, viii, 6, 7, 22-27, 35, 39-41, 43-49, 53-60, 62, 63, 65-68, 70-74, 85, 86, 88-91, 90-93, 95-98, 100, 101, 103-111, 122, 124, 125, 129, 130, 133, 135-140, 142, 143, 151-159, 161, 163-165, 168, 169, 172

Christian Life, vii, 8, 44, 47, 56, 71, 74, 98, 158, 169

Church, vii, ix, 2-6, 16, 18, 40, 42, 53, 55-62, 64-66, 70, 75, 86, 88, 89, 95, 97-100, 102, 104, 111, 122, 125, 127, 133-138, 152, 155, 160, 166, 171, 172

Communion, 5, 56, 58, 59, 98, 121, 133

Community, 11, 29, 56-58, 69, 71, 89, 105, 106, 108, 109, 111, 133, 134, 141, 142, 155, 156, 158-160, 168, 169

Confession, 57, 96, 99, 100, 102, 103, 110, 135, 138, 152, 160-162, 167

Death, 14, 21, 41, 44, 48, 90, 95, 96, 107, 108, 126, 137, 167

Decalogue, 67, 126, 131, 137, 140, 141

Dialogue, 11, 12, 25, 28, 45, 48, 55, 67, 102, 109, 111, 120, 125, 126, 128, 132, 134, 139, 141, 152

Direction, 12, 20, 26, 67, 69, 138, 151

Dynamic, 8, 11, 28, 40, 43, 46-48, 89, 119, 121, 131, 151, 154, 164

Election, 7, 25, 26, 35

Embodiment, 75, 87, 157-159

Eucharist, ix, 40, 60, 101, 102, 165

Eucharistia, 6, 102

Ex Opere Operato, 19, 95, 163

Ex Verbum, 43

Excommunicatio, 97

Faith, vii, ix, 3, 19, 23-26, 35-38, 40, 41, 43-48, 53, 54, 57-61, 63, 64, 68, 74, 85, 90, 91, 93-96, 99-102, 104-108, 110, 123, 125,